"Tony Robinson's *Changing the Conversation* offers real help for pastors and other leaders of local congregations. A fine book, it will provoke discussion and, by God's grace, new zeal for the gospel. Perfect for seminarians who anticipate pastorates and for seminary continuing education events."

— **Louis Weeks**
President Emeritus,
Union Theological Seminary–PSCE

"*Changing the Conversation* provokes church leaders and clergy to engage in courageous work. With clarity and insight Robinson urges those who care about the church to discover a third way to vibrant faith and practice that transcends old polarities. Continuing the groundbreaking work begun in *Transforming Congregational Culture*, Robinson outlines ten essential conversations that can transform, deepen, and sustain the life of every congregation seeking a new heart."

— **Verlee A. Copeland**
Union Church of Hinsdale, Illinois

CHANGING THE CONVERSATION

A Third Way for Congregations

Anthony B. Robinson

WILLIAM B. EERDMANS PUBLISHING COMPANY
GRAND RAPIDS, MICHIGAN / CAMBRIDGE, U.K.

Published 2008 by

Wm. B. Eerdmans Publishing Co.

2140 Oak Industrial Drive N.E., Grand Rapids, Michigan 49505 /

P.O. Box 163, Cambridge CB3 9PU U.K.

Printed in the United States of America

13 12 11   7 6 5 4 3 2

Library of Congress Cataloging-in-Publication Data

Robinson, Anthony B.

    Changing the conversation: a third way for congregations / Anthony B. Robinson.

      p.   cm.

    ISBN 978-0-8028-0759-5 (pbk.: alk. paper)

    1. Church.   2. Church renewal.   I. Title.

    BV600.3.R625   2008

    250 — dc22

2008011995

www.eerdmans.com

Contents

Changing the Conversation: A Third Way for Congregations

Changing the culture of organizations, groups, and institutions — and even societies — is about changing the conversation. Those leading change use new language (or rediscover older language), introduce different topics, formulate new agendas, and offer alternative ways of framing issues and situations. One might understand the Christian faith itself as, in important ways, an ongoing effort at changing the conversation and thus changing the way we understand our lives and the way we live in the world. In the sacrament of baptism we name and rename a child or an adult as "a child of God, a disciple of Christ, and a member of the church." During Lent and Easter we reframe loss and defeat as God's strange way of victory and hope. When we are asked to offer our gifts to God in the practice of offering, we are invited to set aside the dominant languages of consumerism and scarcity and to discover ourselves within a complex narrative of receiving, giving, and abundance. Each Sunday during worship people rename and reframe themselves as they confess their sins, listen as forgiveness is announced, and hear a word from the Lord proclaimed. Churches are ongoing attempts to change the conversation, whether they are our internal and personal conversations or the dominant and conventional ways that matters are construed in North American society.

Change in congregations is also, in significant part, a matter of changing the conversation, and that is my argument in this book. Building on two of my earlier books, including *Transforming Congregational Culture* and *What's Theology Got to Do with It? Convictions, Vitality,*

1

and the Church,[1] I contend that making progress on the challenges before us in the mainline Protestant churches in North America is about changing the conversation. Moreover, it is about having and sustaining ten crucial conversations that are framed in the ten chapters of this book: they constitute an agenda for congregations of the mainline Protestant tradition. My hope is to get us involved in having the conversations that are crucial for the renewal and vitality of our congregations in the twenty-first century.

Congregations are often engaged in conversations that don't go anywhere. Their conversation is stuck because they are not discerning reality accurately and are not framing the challenges adequately. Thus recurrent conversations end up reinforcing a status quo of decline and resignation. Time after time I have seen congregations unwittingly collude in framing their reality and challenges in ways that do not allow them to make progress, indeed, will ensure that things stay much the same. In Conversation 2, I will offer some examples of these kinds of stuck conversations. My point here is that, in order for congregations of the once venerable mainline Protestant tradition to make progress on significant challenges, the movement toward making progress will involve changing the conversation. It will mean discovering new language or perhaps recovering older words and concepts from the living tradition of our faith. New vitality will mean a fresh agenda of subjects; renewal will mean framing our reality more accurately. And vitality and renewal together will mean reframing our present and future in ways that move beyond the predictable but nonproductive conversations.

A Third Way for Congregations

My own call to the ordained ministry came in the early 1970s. Those years were much like the early years of the present century: that is, they were characterized by extreme polarization in North American culture. It was the time of the Vietnam War and the Watergate scandal, and public issues tended to be framed in divisive polarities. At that time I

---

1. See Anthony B. Robinson, *Transforming Congregational Culture* (Grand Rapids: Eerdmans, 2003); see also Robinson, *What's Theology Got to Do with It? Convictions, Vitality, and the Church* (Herndon, VA: Alban Institute, 2006).

was considering a career in higher education and the academy. I opted out of that, at least in part, because the college or university campus often seemed to be just another camp in the cultural wars. I sensed that the way ahead was not to divide and conquer; rather, it was one of seeking and finding common ground. For me, the call to the ministry and congregational leadership was, in good part, the call to a community and tradition that reminded human beings not of what separated us but of what we had and held in common.

In the mid-1970s, when I completed my first professional "Profile," the document that was used in my denomination as part of the pastoral search process, I remember declaring in my Statement on Ministry that I didn't find the categories of "liberal" and "conservative" to be all that helpful. Rather than locate myself in one such camp or the other, I spoke of my enthusiasm for the church, for its rich tradition, and for its work of transforming both lives and communities. I imagined congregations that would enable people to be rooted in vital faith *and* to be engaged in the world. This was a time in the church when those two aspects were often split, with some seeming to emphasize faith and spirituality while others seemed to be oriented toward activism in the community and world. Early in my own ministry I saw the church as a people and community called to bridge and transcend what I saw as false dichotomies, for example, personal transformation and social justice, or spirituality and service among those in need. For me, these were "both/ands," not "either/ors." In that first Statement on Ministry I declined to locate myself in terms of the current polarities, and I expressed my interest in seeking another way.

As I moved into ministry, I continued to imagine the church as a way beyond predictable polarities, beyond the stereotypes and smugness that often accompanied them. This was not always an easy path. It meant that I was emphasizing Christian formation among those who often preferred activism; on the other hand, it meant that I emphasized cultural engagement to those who tended to see their faith as limited to the personal and familial. Many people, including those in congregations, like to put others — perhaps especially clergy — in one category or another. It was my preference to elude and even confound the usual categories. I took Scripture very seriously and was a biblical preacher; but I took social justice very seriously as well. I believed prayer to be important and powerful; but I thought that careful cultural analysis was as well. I wanted to talk about Jesus and about welcoming persons who were gay or lesbian; but I cared about families and what it took to maintain and sustain families. I understood the church to be a new family that transcended categories of race, class, and gender.

Meanwhile, the polarized social script by which our society understands itself became more pronounced as the twentieth century turned into the twenty-first. This script is on display on television screens each election night as the states on the map of the United States are portrayed in either red or blue, with no gradations, shadings, or alternative colors. As issue after issue is framed in terms of polarized alternatives, Americans have become very familiar with the phrase "culture wars." People are either "pro-life" or "pro-choice," either "pro-growth" or "pro-environment," either "pro-peace" or "pro-defense," "creationist" or "evolutionist." The Jesus fish and Darwin fish (with legs) joust with each other on the bumpers of our cars. Who invents this stuff? Who writes this ridiculous script? It may make for highly adrenalized talk radio or television programs where people scream and shout, but it gets us nowhere in terms of making progress on any real challenges. "The culture wars," says Richard Floyd, my fellow pastor and friend, "make us stupid."

Nevertheless, the church is often ensnared in the web of the culture wars and often uses the polarizing rhetoric of our society. There is the Christian Right and the Christian Left, a two-party explanation of Christianity in North America that mirrors the culture wars but also obscures more than it reveals about the complex nature of Christianity and the church in North America. Moreover, this two-party construal blinds us to the emerging possibilities that transgress the usual categories and boundaries. The polarized distinctions of the political Right and Left tend to be mirrored in the churches as evangelical versus liberal, or megachurch versus traditional churches, or emergent versus established. Such distinctions often come to the fore in churches over issues of worship and music: in worship, we have "contemporary" worship pitted against "traditional"; in music, it's praise music versus traditional hymns or classical music. In my current work with a variety of congregations and denominations, I find this narrative to be almost ubiquitous — and equally unhelpful. Indeed, it is often worse: it is destructive.

Is a third way possible? Is there a way beyond the polarized alternatives of either liberal or conservative, left or right, red or blue, traditional or contemporary, praise or classical? And if it is possible, is that third way merely a compromise between extremes, a muddle in the middle, or is it a vital center and a new framing of the conversation?

One recent framing of a vital third way is offered by Diana Butler Bass, a historian of American religion and observer of contemporary Christianity. In her books *The Practicing Congregation* and *Christianity for the Rest of Us,* she writes about congregations that she describes as "intentional" and "comprehensive." Such congregations are not adequately described with the labels "liberal" or "conservative," "left" or "right": they combine intentional Christian practices and Christian formation with service work and an emphasis on social justice. In congregations such as these, says Bass, "church is the sacred space where saints *and* sinners gather to hear God's word, engage practices of prayer and service, and be transformed through participation. There is no spiritual test to come in, no intellectual position to which one must agree. This is the vision of the comprehensive church: a congregation not torn asunder by the riptides of cultural extremism but a place where Christian practices frame all of life and, in the words of the old hymn, 'heal the sin-sick soul.'"[2]

Still others are changing the conversation with other words and descriptions. Princeton missiologist Darrell Guder has written of the "missional church": such a congregation does not view America as a Christian nation but as a context for mission. The congregation is called to be a leavening influence, the yeast in a loaf, and a seasoning salt to the world, to use New Testament images. Guder's missional church cannot be reduced to either liberal or conservative, left or right; it is something new. It is a congregation that relates to its community and setting while taking Christian formation seriously. "The word *mission* means 'sending,' and the church is the primary way in which God's sending is happening," says Guder. "Mission no longer begins when we cross a cultural or national boundary." Mission happens today in the context of a Western society that is "radically secularized."[3]

2. Diana Butler Bass, *Christianity for the Rest of Us* (San Francisco: HarperSanFrancisco, 2006), p. 35.

3. Darrell Guder, "Leadership in New Congregations: New-Church Development from the Perspective of Missional Theology," in *Extraordinary Leaders in Extraordinary Times,* vol. 1: *Unadorned Clay Pot Messengers,* ed. H. Stanley Wood (Grand Rapids: Eerdmans, 2006), pp. 1-29.

Others are contributing their own formulations and language in the search for a third way. Michael Foss, a Lutheran pastor, speaks of developing "a culture of discipleship" in congregations. He describes the central challenge facing Protestant mainline congregations as a paradigm shift from a "culture of membership" to a "culture of discipleship."[4] Like Bass and Guder, Foss moves beyond the old scripts and the tired polarities to envision something new. All three of these writers get their bearings more from Scripture than they do from a polarized cultural script.

Brian McLaren is another person who is looking beyond the usual frameworks toward something new. "Increasing numbers of us have been talking," says McLaren, "about what a post-conservative, post-liberal convergence would look like in the American church. We have become convinced that this convergence would entail the rediscovery of the local church as a missional, disciple-making community engaged in transformative spiritual practices."[5] Elsewhere McLaren writes of what he calls "generous orthodoxy," another attempt to reach for a new language as well as a new reality.[6] The term "generous orthodoxy" suggests a faith and church with a strong center and yet minds and hearts open to the other.

In these third-way congregations, spirituality is real *and* worship is vital, God is alive *and* people are engaged in practicing and expressing faith. That is, they are living their faith in their vocations and relationships, in service and action on behalf of the poor and marginalized. Whether it is Bass's "intentional congregation" or Guder's "missional church" or my own "rooted in faith/engaged in the world," the primary identity of congregations that embody an emerging third way is not either left or right, liberal or conservative, because their primary identity is "Christian." Rather than being Democrat or Republican, their reference points are Scripture, preaching and the sacraments, life in community, and a social critique informed and shaped by all three. They are not churches that care only, or primarily, about *either* personal transformation *or* the public square. They care about both, and they work at both.

---

4. Michael Foss, *Power Surge: Six Marks of Discipleship for a Changing Church* (Minneapolis: Augsburg Fortress, 2000), p. 11.

5. McLaren, quoted in Jeffrey Jones, *Traveling Together* (Herndon, VA: Alban Institute, 2006), p. ix.

6. Brian McLaren, *A Generous Orthodoxy* (Grand Rapids: Zondervan, 2004), p. 23.

Framing a Third Way

As a way of deepening this attempt to suggest a third way, let me draw on two other conceptual frameworks that both suggest the limits of the polarized alternatives in which matters are often framed and point to the qualities of a third way. One such conceptual framework is *set theory*. As I noted in my book *What's Theology Got to Do with It?* set theory enables us to name and differentiate three different kinds of "sets," or social groups or congregations: the open, the bounded, and the centered. I have found that many mainline Protestant congregations have seen their only alternatives as either the bounded or open set, and yet they find the centered option to be both energizing and a better description of the reality of what they are and also of what they seek.

An *open-set* congregation is one where one is likely to hear people say things like, "We're an open congregation — people have all kinds of different beliefs." Or they will say, "You can believe whatever you want to here." "Everyone is welcome, there's no pressure to believe anything" is another way members of an open-set congregation might describe themselves. This kind of congregation can be visually represented as a random bunch of dots on a page, the dots representing different individuals or subgroups. There are no boundaries at all: that is, there are no lines between who belongs and who does not belong. But neither is there any center. Initially, such an open set may appear quite thrilling, even liberating, especially to those who have come from a system or congregation that had very clear and hard boundaries and where they have felt they did not fit in or were subjected to pressures to conform that were uncomfortable. "Isn't it great?" such a newcomer might say. "Here, at this church, we can think and say whatever we want!" But another person, one who has been around longer, might have a different view. She or he might respond: "Like you, I found it wonderful at first. But as time has gone on, it has proved frustrating as well. It's difficult to actually do anything together. And when it comes right down to it, I'm not even sure if we are together or if there is anything we belong to. We just seem to be a collection of individuals, each with his own viewpoint, ideas, and agendas!" Such are the strengths — and the weaknesses — of the open set.

The *bounded-set* congregation is the opposite. Visually, the bounded set has very clear, bold, and heavy boundaries. Visualize a square, rectangle, or circle with some dots (representing individuals or groups) inside and others outside of the line defining the shape of the set. You can easily tell who is in and who is not. The strengths and weaknesses of the bounded set are pretty much the mirror image of the open set. The open set proclaims, "All are welcome here," but some people feel frustrated that there is no "here" here, so to speak: there is nothing really to be part of, no unified group that can work together on shared goals. On the other hand, the bounded set has a clear but possibly confining sense of identity. Such a group does have a clear identity and can pursue common objectives, but there is little openness to difference, and few questions are entertained. If the open set seems inclusive, the bounded set appears exclusive. Often in congregations, conversation about identity seems to pit open and bounded-set options against one another as if no other alternatives exist.

But there is an alternative, a third way. For many congregations, a better choice is to think about their church as — and work toward its becoming — a *centered set.* The centered set may be pictured as having a clear center — for example, a large dot or small circle at the center — but no boundaries; or, if there are boundaries, those boundaries are highly permeable, perhaps a broken line defining inside and outside. Dots representing individuals and groups are scattered around the center. In a centered set the key question, rather than who is in and who is out, is, What direction are you moving in? Are you moving toward the center or away from the center?

In the centered set the task of the congregation, or its leaders, is not so much to police the boundaries as it is to define and articulate its center. "This is who we are and what we are about. You decide if it's right for you." This is the message of the centered-set congregation. In contrast to the open set, the centered set has an identity, a coherent core that gives definition and content to the group or body; in contrast to the bounded set, the focus is not so much on the boundaries, which are permeable, but on the center. Such a centered set allows both identity/purpose and openness. It may be summed up as "strong center/open boundaries." Many congregations will find the centered-set concept helpful in a world in which the extremes of open and bounded sets are both common, and each in their way inadequate. Moreover, the centered-set theory demonstrates conceptually the power of a third way. This third way is more than a compromise between alternatives; it has a vitality and power of its own.

As another demonstration of what might be called "third-way thinking," I wish to draw from Barbara Brown Taylor's exploration in her little book *Speaking of Sin: The Lost Language of Salvation.* The title and subtitle suggest that Taylor's project is to change the conversation by introducing old language (i.e., "sin" and "salvation") but with new or renewed meaning. In the course of her exploration of the meaning of sin, Taylor briefly uses a threefold typology that turns on how different congregations understand and interpret sin. Two of her three types more or less embody the liberal-conservative dichotomies, commonly considered the only available options: the "church-as-clinic" and "church-as-court" options.

The church-as-clinic tends to view sin through a medical lens and to treat it primarily as illness. Such churches operate like clinics, "where sin-sick patients receive sympathetic care for the disease they all share. It is palliative care, for the most part. No one expects anyone to be fully cured, which is why there is not much emphasis on individual sin. Such churches subscribe to a kind of no-fault theology in which no one is re-sponsible because everyone is." If the church-as-clinic is long on com-passion but short on responsibility, the church-as-court type is pretty much the opposite: the lens through which this church views sin is not a medical one but a legal one. Sin, in its view, is crime or lawlessness: "Sins and sinners are named out loud, along with punishments appro-priate to their crimes. On the whole, [however] the sinners identified by this full-fault theology tend to be people who do not belong to the fold."

Those who feel a great need for certainty may gravitate toward the church-as-court, while those who savor acceptance may seek the church-as-clinic. But in reality — that is, when considered in the frame-work of Christian theological conviction — neither one of these by itself really holds up. "True repentance . . . will not work in the church-as-clinic because repentance will not make peace with sin. Instead, it calls individuals to take responsibility for what is wrong in the world — be-ginning with what is wrong with them — and to join with other people who are dedicated to turning things around."

"True repentance," Taylor continues, "will not work in the church-as-courtroom either, because it is not interested in singling out scape-goats and punishing them. Instead, it calls the whole community to en-gage in the work of repair and reconciliation without ever forgetting their own culpability for the ways things are."

While Taylor acknowledges that a third type of church may seem rare, it does exist. Taylor calls this third way a "church-as-community-of-human-transformation." Such a congregation is one where members are expected to be about the business of new life and supported in doing so. "In a life of faith, so conceived, God's grace is not simply the infinite supply of divine forgiveness on which hopeless sinners depend. Grace is also the mysterious strength God lends human beings who commit themselves to the work of transformation."[7] In other words, it is not either compassion or responsibility, either judgment or mercy; it is both, and it is more. It is being about the business of new life, the transformation of individuals and society, and a third way between false, if popular, dichotomies.

Both set theory and Barbara Brown Taylor's depiction of different types of congregations with respect to sin and repentance demonstrate the limits of the usual polarized alternatives and the possibilities of a third way. Both change the given conversation with fresh language, new frameworks, and imaginative possibilities that reveal a way when it seemed there was no way. It is my intention in this book to assist congregations in doing more of this: discovering fresh language, developing new conceptual frameworks, and imagining ways of doing church and being church that are emerging even as I write and as you read.

For some time now, particularly within the last thirty years, many thoughtful people have spoken of our time as transitional: some old concepts and realities — "Christendom" and "modernity" — are ending. But it has not been clear what the shape of their replacements will be. Phyllis Tickle sums it up by observing: "Postmodern, post-Christian, post-Protestant, post-denominational. What do all these posts mean? That we know where we have been but that we have no idea where we are going!"[8]

Nor has it been evident what a new church or new form of church might look like. Some have seized on the megachurch model, from which there is much to be learned. And yet that application also has limits. Others have clung doggedly to something they like to call "traditional." We have not known what might or should emerge. While this

---

7. Barbara Brown Taylor, *Speaking of Sin: The Lost Language of Salvation* (Cambridge, MA: Cowley Publications, 2000), pp. 76-77.

8. Phyllis Tickle, quoted in Bass, *Christianity for the Rest of Us,* p. 22.

process and time of trial will continue, it now seems possible to discern a new future for the old mainline — really a new church for the twenty-first century in North America. It reaches down to our theological roots and to a living tradition. It reaches out to a more diverse culture with a wide embrace. It reaches in toward personal spiritual growth and transformation. It reaches out to a God who goes before us into the world God has made and loves. A new third way is emerging that allows us to move beyond our stereotyped understandings of "liberal" and "conservative," "right" and "left," "contemporary" and "traditional" to a new reality that transcends old polarities.

What's Ahead? An Overview

For congregations that seek such a third way, there are perhaps ten important conversations that they need to initiate, deepen, and sustain in their ongoing life. These conversations are all contributions: they are different elements of the overall effort to change the conversation, particularly in long-established congregations and denominations of the Protestant mainline tradition. They seek to nurture an emerging third way. Here's a thumbnail sketch of the ten conversations that I will encourage in the succeeding chapters. Notice that each chapter has "conversation/reflection prompts" that I hope will stimulate . . . well, conversation! These conversation/reflection prompts are not all found at the end of each chapter, as is traditional in this kind of book. Rather, I have sprinkled them in along the way both to suggest and encourage ongoing reflection and conversation.

It is my hope that this book will be used in denominational and judicatory offices, among their staffs and lay leaders, and that it will also find an audience in seminary classrooms concerned about congregational renewal, congregational leadership, and the future of the church. Most of all, however, I hope this work will be read in congregations, by their leaders and their participants. I would dare to hope that some congregations might use this book in a format that some cities and communities have found popular: "What If All of [name of city] Read the Same Book Together?" This is not just a way for me to sell a few books, though I am not averse to that! It is a way of doing what I am writing about, that is, changing the conversation. When congregation members, or a significant portion of them, read and discuss something together, things happen. They have a common experience that deepens their life together and can enrich their future prospects. All relationships and communities depend on sharing common experiences. For too long our practice in mainline Protestant congregations has been for pastors to go off to some enrichment event or conference, or for clergy to read an important book and tell others about it. Those days are over. We need more formative, common experiences that clergy and parishioners share in our congregations. And we need people to engage each other in the conversation about what God is up to in our time and how we are called to respond.

Conversation 1, "It's Not About You," moves us directly into the subject about what God may be up to in our time. This chapter is intended to help all of us better understand the huge shifts that have occurred in North American culture and their impact on religion, spirituality, and the churches. For some, this focus on the end of the era of American Christendom (note that I say "Christendom," not "Christianity") and the waning of modernity will be familiar; for others, it will be the naming of something they have experienced but have not yet named adequately or helpfully themselves. For still others, it may be the unwelcome description of the end of a known world. In my experience of working with congregations, many pastors and other seminary-educated people have read and thought about the demise of Christendom and of the modern/postmodern shifts, but only a relatively small number of regular, nonclergy church members have done so. The consequence of this is a gap between what ministers perceive and are trying to do and what is perceived by church members for whom such initiatives don't make sense — and may even appear to be disruptive. Conversation 1 takes us to the 10,000-foot level for the big picture.

Lest we get too comfortable with the big picture and the large view, Conversation 2, "And Yet . . . It *Is* About You," brings it all home. Scripture teaches us, and life confirms, that while we may not be in control of what comes our way, how we respond to what confronts us *is* up to us. We are, by God's grace and in God's design, responsible ("responseable"). This second conversation reminds us of our capacity for creative response and suggests some steps and strategies that can help us move beyond lament and complaint, bewilderment and apathy, toward becoming engaged in a creative response to our new time.

But such a movement from lament to praise, a movement that is at the core of so many of the psalms, envisions changed hearts and minds. It entails a new heart, or change and renewal at the center. Too often programs for congregational renewal and vitality remain superficial (by "superficial" I do not mean silly or pointless; I mean that they remain on the surface). They attempt to move the pieces of the organization around, develop new programs or strategies, or change the names and terminology without getting to the heart of the matter. In Conversation 3, "A New Heart," I turn to what seems to me the heart of the matter, the faith experience and the God message. We shall consider the four vessels of a new heart — evangelism, worship, Scripture, and theology — and how they need to be reframed for an emerging third way.

Wherever you find a vital congregation, you find strong and capable leadership. Once we've said that, however, there is no clear agreement about what is meant by "strong and capable leadership." "Who Shall Lead Them?" is the title of Conversation 4, which invites us into a discussion about the nature of leadership, the functions of leaders, and different leadership roles in congregations. I argue that, during the Christendom period, clergy were often prepared for roles as chaplains and scholars, but they were not always prepared to be congregational leaders. Moreover, the strong emphasis on pastoral care in seminary education for a generation or two now may have come at the expense of leadership. Our new time places a premium on developing leadership capacity, not only among ordained ministers but also in the church as a whole.

Perhaps the most important conversation fostered by capable leaders is the conversation about purpose, which is the focus of Conversation 5, "Why Are We Here?" In far too many long-established congregations, the de facto purpose has become maintaining themselves. The question that is not asked or answered is: For what? To what end? What is our purpose as a church? And would someone be able to tell if that purpose were being accomplished or not? A Seattle microbrewery named Hale's Ales, whose product I enjoy, has as its advertising mantra: "The main thing is to keep the main thing the main thing!" What is our main thing in the church? If we know what it is, are we keeping it at the center of our thoughts, activities, and prayers?

When effective leaders have fostered a deep and serious conversation about purpose and have come to some biblically grounded, community-supported clarity about it, Conversation 6, "Write the Vision," asks the question, What's next? or What does the Lord require of us? Borrowing from Ron Heifetz, a teacher of leadership, I call this "taking on adaptive challenges." Adaptive challenges are the key challenges before a congregation that wishes to more fully realize and fulfill its purpose and potential. Not every congregation faces the same adaptive challenges, so discernment is called for. For one congregation a crucial piece of adaptive work will be to make progress on its ministry of adult Christian formation. For another congregation the adaptive work that seems urgent may be to make the shift from a "board culture" to a "ministry culture." Yet another congregation's adaptive work may entail a move away from stewardship as simply "making the budget" to growing congregations of generous people and stewardship as a spiritual practice. I offer some examples of adaptive challenges and adaptive work to make sure this conversation is well grounded in reality. Conversation 7 is devoted to a particular adaptive challenge with which many today struggle: governance and organization.

One other sort of adaptive work is so crucial for mainline Protestant congregations that I want to single it out as a conversation of its own: Conversation 8 is about "The Church and the Public Square." There was a time, in the memory of some still living, when the public square was, if not owned, then dominated by mainline Protestants. As we stood proudly and sometimes literally on the public squares of North American towns and cities, our role as moral custodians was often taken for granted. That, along with much else, has now changed. How are mainline Protestants to play a role in the public conversation about morality and society, justice and the common good, spiritual values and a new commons? The Religious Right has seized on one option: they declare that America is a Christian nation and that Christians and their views ought to hold the privileged and dominant place. At least partly in response to this way of being in the public square, many mainline Christians seem to have become tongue-tied and marginalized. That is to say, either there is a new kind of triumphalism embodied by the Religious Right or there is a bewildered quietism embodied by mainline congregations and denominations. Neither of these two options is faithful to our own best lights or to the needs of our times. We need to talk about this particular adaptive challenge in thoughtful and fresh ways.

While I aim in this book to contribute to the renewal of the church, particularly that portion of the church known as mainline Protestantism, not all congregations will be capable of or successful at renewal efforts. For some — and in some ways for all — there is another important conversation that I open in Conversation 9: "Death and Resurrection." For Christians, death is not the end; indeed, it may be the prelude to a new beginning. There are situations where God may be calling congregations to a graceful and gracious ending and death, in order that resurrection can come. In this conversation I consider some examples and stories of death and resurrection that remind us that death is not the end for us, and that surprising new life is possible.

Finally, Conversation 10 explores the question "Where do we start?" For some congregations, perhaps those in the midst of a pastoral search process, getting clear about the role of leadership is the critical next step. For others, a back-to-the-basics focus on the first two conversations may be the beginning point. For many, that work will already have taken place, and they are ready to move their focus to "purpose" and "vision." Still others are ripe for a conversation about death and resurrection. In the final conversation, I attempt to help congregations know where and how to take their next step.

Is this list of ten conversations a priority list, the first being the most important and the tenth being the least important? No. All of them seem important to me, though perhaps the first four are the most fundamental. If not a list in priority of importance, are the ten conversations then sequential, one leading to another and thus to be taken in sequence? They are sequential and can be approached in a sequential way; but congregational life is seldom neat, tidy, or sequential, and you may find yourself jumping around or having more than one conversation at a time. Finally, are these ten conversations the only ten conversations that one might have as we seek to change the conversation and discover a third way for congregations? No. I'm sure there are other important conversations of which you are aware or which you will discover. However, these ten have emerged from my work as a congregational leader, teacher, and speaker in a variety of settings, and as a congregational consultant and coach to leaders. Since *Transforming Congregational Culture* was published in 2003, I have had the privilege of working with a great number of congregations and clergy across North America, in eight different denominations, and in churches of varying sizes and settings. This book reflects that work and what I have learned with you and from you. Therefore, it is an act and expression of gratitude to my readers and publishers, to my teachers and students, to my own congregations and all the congregations with whom I have been privileged to work. In the end, of course, our deepest gratitude is to God: "For from him and through him and to him are all things. To God be the glory forever. Amen" (Rom. 11:36).

It's Not About You

You may recall the enormous sense of relief you felt as you talked with someone who was in a difficult or discouraging situation that bore resemblances to your own. "I guess I'm not the only one," you thought to yourself, or "Maybe I'm not crazy after all." These are the kinds of things we feel when another parent confides her anxieties about the behaviors of her four-year-old, and they sound exactly like what we had been thinking were the sure signs that our own four-year-old was destined for life as a criminal sociopath. Or we may experience a similar sense of relief when we hear from someone who, like us, is in the midst of job search and has come to the conclusion that he will never be hired — or even seriously considered — by any employer in the known world ever again. Suffering tends to isolate us; but sharing our stories with others and hearing their stories overcomes the isolation, alleviates the fear that something is uniquely wrong with us, and provides us both perspective and hope.

Sometimes when I work with congregations and leaders who are struggling with mighty challenges and have little that they can point to as evidence of success, I get the sense that I am talking to people who think they have the world's worst and most uniquely hopeless situation. Not only do they believe that they are the only ones; worse, they believe that they are to blame. This applies to ordained clergy and to concerned laity who are very close to concluding that "it must just be me," or "it must be us." But it's not about you. You and I find ourselves trying to lead and love congregations in the time of a sea change.

What shall we do? The first step for many congregations and their leaders is to gain an understanding of the large changes and challenges that congregations in North America, particularly in the mainline traditions, are facing. Because these shifts are so large and so deep, this is no small task. But it is a critically important one. Another way of putting this is that a key next step for leaders is to help the congregations they lead gain an accurate picture of reality. Lovett Weems, a teacher of church leadership, puts it this way: "The key question is, 'What is the nature of the situation in which we find ourselves?' Anything less is inadequate as a basis for next steps. Once there is a correct definition of reality, then, and only then, can planning begin regarding appropriate next actions."[1] That is, when we get an accurate read on what's going on, when we define the reality of our situation, we will discover that it's not all about us. There are large forces at work. In many ways that is simply the way it is, and it's not anyone's fault: we are in the midst of cultural sea change.

The term "sea change" comes, as my colleague Martin Copenhaver notes in a book we did together, from Shakespeare's *The Tempest*, where Ariel sings:

"Nothing of him doth fade
But doth suffer a sea-change
Into something rich and strange."

Copenhaver observes: "Much of the time it can seem that the church we love is merely fading away, but those of us who cling to the promise of the Resurrection already know that God has a way of taking the raw stuff of decay, and even of death, and fashioning it into something 'rich and strange.' This God is not finished yet. And so, I believe, neither is the church."[2]

A sea change is what is going on now in North American religion. And just as neither you nor I cause the tides to ebb or flow, this is not really about you or me or us. That is, these are shifts and changes — sea changes — that we did not cause. Instead of blaming these changes on ourselves or on others, we would do better to try to identify and de-

1. Lovett Weems, *Taking the Next Step* (Nashville: Abingdon, 2003), p. 41.
2. Martin Copenhaver, Anthony Robinson, and William Willimon, *Good News in Exile* (Grand Rapids: Eerdmans, 1997), p. 12.

scribe them, understand them, and frame them in ways that give us a chance to respond to them — to catch a wave rather than being crushed by one. In this chapter I will try to describe the sea change in which we find ourselves.

We're Not in Kansas, Toto

One of the most memorable lines from any movie comes from the 1939 classic *The Wizard of Oz*, when Dorothy looks with astonishment around the new place to which a tornado has delivered her and says to her dog, "Toto, I've a feeling we're not in Kansas anymore." Many people in congregations have a similar feeling. We sense that we are no longer on known turf, but we can't always name exactly what's changed or where we are now. One important way to describe what has changed is to say that Western and American Christendom are over. Again, I ask the reader to note carefully that I did not say that "Christianity" is over, but that "Christendom" is finished. There is a difference.

What was Christendom? As a word, "Christendom" is the combination of two words: *Christ* and *dominion* (which can be defined as "rule," "governance," or "establishment"). It is important to remind ourselves that Christianity existed before Christendom: that is, Christianity was not always linked to the governing powers, to those who reigned, or to the establishment. In fact, in its first three centuries in the Western world, Christianity had a tense relationship with the societies that surrounded it and with the ruling powers of the Roman world. Sometimes Christians were persecuted, sometimes they were ignored, but one thing was clear: in those first three centuries the early church of Christians was not in society's driver's seat. That changed in the early fourth century, when Rome's Emperor Constantine embraced Christianity and declared the Christian faith to be the official religion of the Roman Empire, which in time became known as the Holy Roman Empire (note the amalgamation of church and state in that very name change).

This is a familiar bit of history, so familiar that many of us may have nodded and not paid adequate attention to its enormous implications for church and culture. Think about going to bed one night as a little-known community activist and waking up the next day as a United States senator or having an office in the West Wing! Consider what it might be like to go from being regarded with disdain and suspicion by society's movers and shakers on Thursday to being their darling and confidante the following Monday. Christendom did not happen that fast, of course, but you get the idea. From the margins of Roman society to the center, from legally banned to legally mandated, from the faith of a suspect minority to the religion of an empire. Now that was a sea change!

A subsequent emperor, Charlemagne, would divide the Holy Roman Empire (what became known as Europe) into geographical parishes, each with a parish church and a parish priest. Above the parishes was the cathedral, the seat of the bishop, who oversaw and appointed the priests. Above the bishops was the pope, who was analogous to the emperor in the political realm. All citizens who were within earshot of the bells of the parish church were part of the church simply by virtue of living where they lived. The task of the church and the priest was to see to the religious needs of the people in the parish, which sometimes meant enforcing the will of the people in power, whether it was the emperor or the pope. To a great extent, the focus of the ministry of parish priests in the medieval period was on death, what followed death, and whether a person would be in the right place — or the wrong one — after he or she died. The role of the people in their relationship to the church was to support their parish church, their parish priest, and the hierarchy of the church, which was connected to the hierarchy of the state. Mission meant sending priests and soldiers to lands and peoples outside the boundary of the empire so that they might conquer new territories and peoples for "Christ and the King."

Christendom, despite some significant changes over the centuries, is so familiar to many of us that it is difficult to see what a huge change it was from both the early Christian narrative in Scripture and the era of the early church. Note some of the key changes that came with Christendom. Instead of being focused on congregations, the Christianity of Christendom became a *territorial reality,* which explains the term "local church." In Christendom (and in our Christian culture) residents had their local church in much the same way that they had their local market or provincial law court. It was an established social institution with the assigned task of seeing to the religious part of life.

Mission, instead of being about making disciples and forming new communities of faith as described in the book of Acts and the letters of the New Testament, was about *territorial expansion:* conquering new lands and people and making them "Christian." Meanwhile, at home — that is, within the boundaries of Christendom — the role of the church was to take care of its members; and the members' obligation, in turn, was to maintain their local church. By and large, the work of the church fell to religious professionals: priests, nuns, and members of religious groups and orders. Finally, as Darrell Guder, one of the most perceptive analysts of Christendom, observes: "The church as an institution, [came] to be identified with Western culture: people speak of the United States or European countries as 'Christian nations.' There is a subtle assumption at work that the Western church really represents the kingdom of God as Christ intended it and that our traditions and institutions constitute 'normative Christianity.'"[3]

We can sum up the effects of Christendom by noting the following shifts in key categories:

1. *Conversion and formation* declined because a person was Christian by virtue of citizenship, birth, and residence. This meant that the Christian faith was a social given rather than a choice or conscious commitment.

2. Christianity no longer found its primary embodiment in *congregations,* but in *territories* and *nations.*

3. *Mission* was not an inherent characteristic of every congregation that belonged to all its members; rather, mission was something done by specially designated "missionaries" in territories or nations that were not Christian.

4. The *purpose* of a church was to provide religious services to a particular local population.

5. The ministry of the church increasingly was performed by and belonged to *religious professionals,* whose role was in many ways comparable to that of civil servants or government officials.

6. *Society* (or culture) and *faith* (Christianity) *overlapped* to such an extent that being a good Christian and being a good citizen were equivalent, and each defined the other.

3. Guder, "Leadership in New Congregations: New-Church Development from the Perspective of Missional Theology," in *Extraordinary Leaders in Extraordinary Times,* vol. 1: *Unadorned Clay Pot Messengers,* ed. H. Stanley Wood (Grand Rapids: Eerdmans, 2006), p. 12.

My point is not to say that Christendom was bad or wrong, although it was a significant departure from both the New Testament church and the experience of churches and Christians during the first three centuries. Christendom, or what some refer to as "the Constantinian project," was in many ways an incredible achievement. Through it Christian symbols and values shaped an entire civilization and many nations. It built colleges and universities, founded hospitals and welfare institutions, shaped the arts, and influenced government and economy. Christendom endured, in different variations and iterations, for nearly sixteen centuries in the West, which is a very long run by any measure.

In North America, with the colonization of what became the United States and Canada, Christendom continued, though in a unique form. In Western Europe, Christendom had become embodied in the actual alliance of church and state: state-sponsored and state-supported churches. Even today, if you live in some European countries, you pay taxes to support the established church. In North America, however, a legal separation of church and state was one of the founding principles of the Bill of Rights, and that became a national reality with the end of the last legal establishment of religion in the late 1700s. Nevertheless, Christendom persisted in the United States and Canada, not so much as a legal arrangement or establishment, but as a cultural one. Church and culture were interwoven and mutually supportive in many and varied ways, including the social recognition and support for the Christian day of worship and Christian holidays, ritual use of the Bible on public occasions such as inaugurations and courts of law, privileged access to power and place by religious leaders, Christian influence in public schools and higher education, and much more.

Moreover — and this is a crucial point — the church groups (or denominations) in North America that were born out of the Protestant Reformation in Europe gained the upper hand in the new world, and they, rather than the Roman Catholic Church, became the religious establishment of the new nation. Therefore, these groups are often referred to as "mainline" or "mainstream" Christian churches. Instead of the local parish system of Christendom that was typical in Western Europe, in North America there tended to be the local Presbyterian, Episcopal, Congregational, Baptist, Lutheran, or Methodist church. The territorial or parish system persisted, but with a new denominational shape. Much else remained the same. Mission was "away," somewhere out on the frontier, and in time overseas, or it represented charitable work at home. Local churches provided religious services to their members, and the service providers were professionals (seminary trained and ordained). A person was Christian by virtue of being born in America, "a Christian nation," but was part of a particular tribe or subgroup (i.e., denomination) that often had historical, cultural/linguistic, and socioeconomic characteristics. Religious leaders doubled as social and civic leaders. Being a "good Christian" and a "good American" were quite similar in American Christendom, and Western culture and Christianity were equivalent.

It was a good world in many ways, and Christendom accomplished a great deal that was valuable. There were, to be sure, some problems. Christians of different races and cultures tended not to worship together. African-Americans, for example, were not welcomed into the churches of European-Americans. Nor were sinners and outcasts, those who were apparently Jesus' idea of people to welcome and spend time with, often welcomed into the churches, which functioned as society's moral custodian. The "real" Christians were seminary-trained professionals. Church was something we church members came to think of as "for us": "our church" provided for our religious needs, offering appropriate rituals at the time of birth, puberty, marriage, and death, while mission was something that was done "for others." The purpose for which churches existed had a lot to do with maintaining social order as well as maintaining their own existence and institutional strength and power. We would have been hard put to describe the differences between the Christian faith and the norms and values of Western culture or to identify places where the two were in conflict or even tension.

When the Sea Changed and How

So what happened? One historian of religion in America, Diana Butler Bass, says that the process of Christendom's decline was a gradual one, though it had three distinct phases of "disestablishment."[4] The first disestablishment began in 1789, when the adoption of the Bill of Rights le-

4. Diana Butler Bass, *The Practicing Congregation* (Herndon, VA: Alban Institute, 2004), p. 24.

gally forbade the federal government of the new nation from creating or supporting a single national church; and by 1820 the last legal establishment of Christianity in the United States had ended. However, as I have noted above, this did not mean that an informal religious establishment ceased to exist or was no longer a goal. Moreover, this informal establishment was a mainline Protestant one. As another historian notes, "Protestants conceived of an American Christian democracy infused by their church traditions. . . . [E]verything was geared to protect white Anglo-Saxon Protestant civilization. The arts, economics, politics, even war, bore the Protestant imprint."[5]

According to Bass, the second disestablishment came in the early twentieth century, when the informal Protestant establishment was challenged to include the broader participation of Jews and Roman Catholics. This entailed a shift away from "a distinctly Protestant national identity to a Judeo-Christian one, whereby a generalized sense of monotheistic faith replaced specific Protestant authority as the moral custodian of the nation." Finally, a third disestablishment has been underway since the 1960s. "In this phase, all organized belief — especially traditional Western religion — has been dislodged even as a custodian of national morality and ethics — replaced instead by the authority of the autonomous individual."[6] Another way to put that is to say that authority has shifted from external norms and institutional embodiments to internal and individual ones. True, there are people and communities who say, as one bumper-sticker-sized assertion of external authority has it, "God said it, I believe it, and that settles it." But in many ways this is a reaction against the dominant social ethos, which is perhaps captured in another bumper sticker: "Question Authority." The point is that there has been a gradual dissolution of that informal American and Protestant Christendom: another word for this process is "secularization." Today the United States is an officially secular society where there is not only no *de jure* establishment of religion, but no *de facto* one either. This varies somewhat depending on the region of the nation where you find yourself, with some regions being more overtly secular and others less so. But the point remains: Christendom is by and large over.

Of course, this gradual, three-stage disestablishment is not the only

5. Eldon G. Ernst, quoted in Bass, *Practicing Congregation*, p. 111 n. 4.
6. Bass, *Practicing Congregation*, p. 24.

way to explain the sea change, nor are these shifts the only factors contributing to it. A very significant additional factor has been the immigration to the United States of people whose religious faiths and cultural backgrounds are neither Christian nor part of the Protestant-Catholic-Jew accommodation of the second disestablishment. Especially since the reform of U.S. immigration laws in 1965, there has been a growing presence in North America of not only Orthodox Christians, but also Buddhists, Muslims, and Hindus. In fact, today in some urban areas Muslims outnumber Presbyterians and there are more Buddhists than Methodists — facts that would have astonished my Protestant grandmother. Instead of reading about Muslims and Hindus in textbooks, a growing number of Americans can talk to their neighbors down the street who *are* Muslims or Buddhists. The idea that America is a "Christian nation" has become more difficult to sustain.

This movement toward becoming a religiously pluralistic society has been furthered not only by immigration to the United States but also by a new menu of homegrown religious and spiritual options. Many have remarked on and chronicled the advent of the religious and spiritual "seeker" and the dizzying variety of new religious forms and practices that have responded to spiritual seekers. These new forms range from organized institutions, such as Centers for Spiritual Life, Unity Churches, and Transcendental Meditation Centers, to a wide embrace of various practices of meditation, chanting, drumming, prayer, and mystical exploration. The explosion of spirituality and spiritual seeking reflects the shift of the "third disestablishment": from external norms and their institutional embodiments to authority located in individuals and their choices. The result is a religiously pluralistic society that has many religious and spiritual options on the menu, indeed, so many that it can seem bewildering.

In this dazzling array of choices, the religious world reflects another change in North American culture. In the last one hundred years, our society has shifted from one of local economies based in an agricultural and industrial nation to a consumer economy that is part of a global network and its markets. Just as consumers have a huge array of choices, and the value of choice is part and parcel of the contemporary ethos, so in the area of religion we have — and expect to have — many choices. Fewer people are part of a church or a faith simply because their parents or grandparents were.

In summary, the key factors in the religious sea change have been: (1) the gradual disestablishment of Protestant Christianity and the emergence of an officially secular society; (2) the growth in North America of other religions and the emergence of a religiously and culturally pluralistic society; and (3) the infusion of a consumer ethos — and with it, choice — into the area of religion and spirituality, resulting in the emergence of a large and ever-changing menu of spiritual choices. All in all, we're not in Kansas anymore!

For Reflection and Discussion
- Name one characteristic or aspect of American Christendom that you valued, the loss of which you now grieve.
- Picture a spectrum with "inherited faith" at one end and "chosen faith" at the other. Where would you locate yourself on that spectrum?

So What?

Although I was born in Oregon and live today in Seattle, I spent my childhood in the Washington, D.C., suburb of Arlington, Virginia, during the decades of the 1950s and 1960s. I remember that one couple who were close friends of my parents did not go to church, and this seemed odd to me. In fact, it *was* odd. Almost everyone else we knew went to some church. To ask someone in that era, "What church do you belong to?" would have been just as ordinary a conversational question as asking, "What school do your kids attend?" Today, in Seattle, 13 percent of the population goes to some church, temple, or synagogue in a given week. If you were to ask a new acquaintance in Seattle, out of the blue, "What church do you go to?" you would risk misunderstanding, peculiar looks, even suspicion. In most of the Northwest today, going to church, while certainly not unheard of, is the exception rather than the rule.

I remember when, in the late 1970s, a young woman of perhaps twenty or so said something to me that included the words "when I became a Christian," it was the first time I had heard that. Even at that late date, the words sounded strange to me. When you grew up in Christendom, you did not "become" a Christian. Everyone (except Jews) was a Christian. We might try to be better Christians. But "when I became a

Christian" sounded strange — even arrogant — to my Christendom-attuned ears, as if she had said, "When I attained enlightenment." Now I see Rhonda, that young woman who had grown up in a secular family in the secular Northwest to which I returned in my late twenties, as a harbinger of a new world and someone sent to teach me something. She had chosen a faith of her own rather than inheriting faith as part of the culture, family, and society that had reared her. Quite possibly, choosing faith — becoming a Christian — was a way of being different and at odds with both the general society and her family as well. Rebellion no longer meant, as in Christendom, declaring oneself to be an atheist or an agnostic; rebelling could be declaring oneself to be a Christian, and not a nominal one but a converted one.

These recollections help me answer the "so what?" question. There are many implications of this sea change from American Christendom to the officially secular and religiously and culturally pluralistic society in which we live today. A crucial one is that we can no longer assume that people are Christian by virtue of growing up here in North America. Increasingly today, faith is chosen rather than inherited. This means that churches that once paid little attention to matters of conversion, public commitment, personal transformation, and Christian formation have now been challenged to find ways to address such matters. We need to learn to pay attention to how the gospel changes people; we need to figure out ways in which people can move from nominal faith, or no faith, to a more deeply committed and meaningful faith; and we need to explore the ways in which believers can touch, heal, and change people and communities even as they themselves are touched, healed, and changed by God's love and grace, and by the Christian message.

Another way to put this, and to build on it, is to say that the *purpose* of the church has shifted. During Christendom the purposes of the church included: (1) being the conscience of the community; (2) serving as the instrument of aid to the less fortunate; and (3) being the center of family and community life.[7] All of these made sense in their time, and they all persist in some ways; but none of them are fully adequate depictions of the purpose of the church for this new time. Today the purpose of the church is closer to that of the pre-Constantinian era: the church

---

7. Robinson, *Transforming Congregational Culture* (Grand Rapids: Eerdmans, 2003), pp. 25-30.

exists to change lives. We are in the business of teaching and living a particular way of life. The church's purpose is to be and to make disciples of Jesus Christ for the sake of the world. Having said that, I must add that there is no one way to be a disciple, or follower, of Jesus. We do not have a predetermined outcome or mold, but we do have a direction and a purpose. Churches exist to grow people of faith.

This means that the primary mission of the church is not overseas, nor can it be reduced to charitable work. The primary mission of the church is to change lives, to be and to form disciples for the sake of God's world. This means — and this is a key idea — that the church is itself, in Darrell Guder's term, "missional."[8] Everything the church does and is needs to embody the mission of the church to be witnesses in word and deed to Jesus Christ. It is all about growing people of faith for the sake of the world.

This shift has yet another implication. If the church is missional to its very core and being, and its primary purpose is to change lives and to grow people of faith who are disciples of Jesus for the sake of the world, then we can no longer think of the church as "for us" and mission as "for others." That is no longer a helpful framework, description, or division. The church, our church, is not "ours." It is God's church, called to be an instrument of God's mission of healing and mending God's creation.

A final "so what" has to do with the role of the ordained clergy — the pastors, ministers, and priests. During the Christendom era and in the churches it formed, the ordained and professional clergy tended to be thought of as the locus of spirituality and the channel of a relationship with God. If there was a religious need or spiritual crisis, one called on the minister. If prayer was required, one asked the pastor to pray. If the performance of ritual was called for, one went to priest for the necessary ritual. In public, pastors and priests functioned as moral models, even in a sense moral police, around whom we would "clean up our act," watch our language, or slip the beer bottle behind the couch. Pastors, priests, and chaplains were, most of all, chaplains to the people of a congregation or parish who provided for the religious needs of its people and, to a significant degree, the religious needs of the entire community. Even the Reformation, for all its emphasis on the priest-

---

8. Darrell Guder, *The Continuing Conversion of the Church* (Grand Rapids: Eerdmans, 2000), pp. 52-53.

hood of all believers, did not change that much, if at all. The Christendom model of the local priest or pastor as a chaplain who provides for the religious needs of the members of the church or parish prevailed.

I recall my interview with the pastoral search committee of the first congregation I served after I graduated from seminary. The interview seemed to be going reasonably well when committee members began to enumerate the many ways that they imagined their pastor would participate in the wider community as an embodiment of Christian values and virtues. They hoped that their minister would be involved at the senior center, would attract the town's troubled youth, might possibly serve on the city planning commission, and would generally embody a wholesome Christian witness from one end of town to the other. Daunted by their long list of aspirations they had for their pastor, I gulped and said, "Excuse me, I need to be clear with you about something." I said that I was very interested in "being a Christian *with* you, but I am not interested in being a Christian *for* you." At that moment I had — pretty much unwittingly — put my finger on the fading structure of Christendom, in which an ordained minister was the channel for the things of God and the spirit and was to embody Christianity on behalf of others.

However, if the purpose of the church in our new time is to change lives and grow people of faith for the sake of the world's healing, the minister/priest/pastor is no longer the primary or exclusive God-person or God-channel, nor is he or she the chaplain who provides all religious meaning and services to a congregation's members and to the wider community. Every baptized Christian is a God-person and God-channel, at least potentially. The mission and witness belong to the community of faith, the congregation, and not exclusively to the ordained.

Will we still need ordained people in the emerging world and church? I'm not sure. What I am sure of is that their role will be different. Increasingly, they will be teachers of the faith and mentors in ministry; they will be leaders of congregations. Instead of being chaplains to church and community, they will be congregational leaders and spiritual directors. They will not do most or all of their ministry on behalf of the larger church. They will support that ministry through preaching and teaching, mentoring and guiding.

Just as the sea change is big, the "so what?" is huge. To sum up, let me list the key "so what's":

- a new and renewed emphasis on life change, transformation, or conversion, as well as ongoing Christian formation;
- a change in the primary purpose of the church;
- a shift of mission from "over there" to "right here"
- no longer thinking of the church as "for us" and mission as "for others," but understanding the church itself as a missional body for the sake of the world God created and loves;
- and a shift away from over-reliance on professionally trained and ordained clergy as the locus of ministry and channel of grace. These are huge changes, and we're not done yet.

For Reflection and Discussion
- Do a free association with the word "mission." What words/images/ people come to mind when you hear "mission"?
- Name one exciting opportunity you see hidden in the death of Christendom.

More on the Sea Change

I'm no authority on oceans, but when I am sea kayaking, which is something I love to do, I have noticed that in a particular sea or body of water, there are streams or currents. There are places in the Pacific Ocean's waters in the Puget Sound, for example, where it seems as if there's a river running through the sound's waters. You'll be paddling along in your kayak when suddenly there's a channel or stream in the sea, moving as swiftly as a river in the Cascade Mountains, the mountains that you can see over your shoulder on a clear day.

If the sea we've been paddling in is something like Christendom and that sea has changed, there is a particular stream or channel that has run though it for roughly the last 500 years and has shaped our understanding and living of Christianity in the Christendom sea during that period. This powerful current is *modernity.*

Christendom was born in the closing centuries of the ancient world, the world of Greco-Roman culture. Christendom flourished in the medieval period, which might be thought of as roughly 500 to 1500. But the Protestant churches, the ones that led the way and played the predominant role in American Christendom, came into being and were shaped by modernity, the period that may be thought of as roughly 1500 to 2000. These century designations are all, of course, broad approximations and generalizations. But the point is that the powerful stream of modernity ran into the sea of Western culture and Christendom concurrent with the Protestant Reformation and the churches and denominations it spawned. We need to understand the modern age because modernity shaped these churches; but we also need to understand it because, like Christendom, modernity is in many ways finished now. It is still there and in some ways is still significant, but the powerful current of modernity is no longer running as strong or deep as it did for five hundred years. There are a host of new and different currents and streams running into our sea, the currents and streams of postmodernity.

The differences between the modern and postmodern eras are signaled by changes in a variety of categories and hallmarks, which include but are not limited to communication, economic organization, worldview, intellectual elites, military practices, and forms of transportation.[9] The communication technology of modernity was the printing press; in postmodernity it has been radio and television, but most of all the computer and the internet. The economic organization of modernity replaced feudalism with capitalism, but in our postmodern era a new global economy is upon us. Newton, Descartes, and Kant, among others, provided the intellectual superstructure of modernity, while a new intellectual elite, philosophers such as Derrida, Foucault, and Rorty, the definers and articulators of postmodernity, guide a new worldview and lead the critique of old authorities and worldviews. If the transportation innovation of modernity was the great sailing ship, which made possible the exploration of new territories and continents, the transportation technology of the postmodern world is global air travel, which has had the effect of shrinking the planet and bringing very different cultures into new and rapid proximity. Postmodernity even extends to the military. The wars of modernity consisted of great armies using newly invented guns as they fought over territory. Today, more alarmingly, aerial warfare with laser weaponry and computer-guided combat have changed the face of war and of the military, as has terrorism, which knows no national boundaries.

9. Brian McLaren, *A New Kind of Christian* (San Francisco: Jossey-Bass, 2001), pp. 29ff.

However, the shift from modernity to postmodernity, which in time will probably have a name all its own — not simply "post-modern" — is not merely a matter of technologies, structures, and organizational forms; it is also a matter of values and guiding ideas. Modernity saw *reason* and rational thought as the primary human faculty and way of knowing. Through reason and its expression in science and its application in technology, moderns hoped to gain control over the complexities and vicissitudes of nature and to solve humanity's vexing problems, such as poverty and disease. Because of these heady new capacities, modernity tended to be highly *optimistic,* as it imagined a new world of leisure and luxury for all just around the historical corner.

Other qualities and values beyond reason and optimism marked modernity as well: *universality, objectivity,* and confidence in a *grand narrative,* or story. As the quintessentially modern nation, the United States was seen as a "melting pot," a place where the local and particular were overcome in the embrace of a universal and modern humanity, unencumbered by the traditions and superstitions of the past. Furthermore, moderns tended to believe that objectivity was both desirable and, more important, achievable. We moderns could objectively study, comprehend, and explain the universe and its mysteries. All of this modern ethos was wrapped in the grand narrative of conquest, control, and progress: conquest and control of nature and the unknown and progress in gaining control of our destiny, as well as achieving security and prosperity.

Postmodernity can be understood, at least in part, as a severe critique of all of the values and markers — that is, the ethos — of modernity. Reason and rationality are no longer the only ways of knowing. Postmoderns tend to say, "Speak to us from your heart, not just your head." Postmoderns want to *experience* mystery rather than explain it. They are not as confident of human objectivity because they tend to see everyone as shaped by the context of their culture and experiences: that is, everyone is "coming from" somewhere. The melting pot of universality has given way to a new fascination with the local and the particular, a concentration on the variety of cultures and worldviews. Postmoderns do not share modernity's confidence or optimism that nature will be, or should be, subjected to human control or that progress is inevitable and always good. The great metanarrative of progress and conquest has run aground on the shoals of environmental concern and a loss of confidence in science and technology as reliable sources of our salvation. Instead of a single unifying story or grand narrative, postmodernity sees a world of many stories.

You may be saying, "All of this is very interesting, but what does it have to do with the church and its future?" In a nutshell this: over the last five hundred years Christianity has been defined by its attempts to navigate the currents of modernity. One might say that theological liberalism has been the attempt to make Christianity fit the modern world's structures and values. Theological fundamentalism or conservatism, on the other hand, might be understood as a movement of resistance against modernity. Despite that, however, fundamentalism has also accommodated its views to the currents of modernity in its own ways, and has even granted authority to modernity and its norms.

Since my primary focus in this book is on mainline Protestant churches and denominations, let me dwell a bit on the implications of the powerful stream of modernity for those groups and churches. While there are considerable nuances and variations among those groups, most mainline Protestant bodies did attempt to find at least a truce with modernity, if not to forge an alliance with it. But this did not come without a cost. Although modernity liberated people in many ways, freeing them from the rigidities and authorities of the medieval world, it tended to reduce the human experience in other ways. The modern era tended to eclipse and disdain the nonrational, the spiritual, the mysterious, and the miraculous. The result was a version of Christianity that prized morality but often severely limited spirituality.

Phyllis Tickle has helpfully observed that all religions consist of three major components: spirituality, morality, and corporeality. By "corporeality" she means the physical and institutional expressions of a religion: its buildings, organizational structures, and so on. During Christendom and modernity, the moral and the corporeal (institutional) aspects of religion flourished, but spirituality did not.[10] In its efforts to make Christianity fit the rational, objective, optimistic, and universal world of modernity, the mainline church, at least in some cases, diminished or altogether lost that third aspect of religions — spirituality. Christianity took shape in great institutional churches and nation-

---

10. Phyllis Tickle, *Greed: The Seven Deadly Sins* (New York: Oxford University Press, 2004), pp. 1-2.

ally organized and structured denominations, and in the other institutions they spawned: colleges and universities, health and welfare institutions, and other cornerstones of civic life. Christianity and its leaders were often the moral voices and primary moral influences and custodians of the culture. But the churches, with some exceptions, were not centers of mystery or miracle, of religious ecstasy, or even of religious experience. (A poll conducted not too many years ago indicated that a high percentage of people had experienced something they described as a "miracle" or a direct experience of God's presence. When asked whether they had shared it with their priest or minister, most of them answered in the negative, because they doubted that they would be believed or taken seriously!)

Once again we come to the "so what?" question. On one level, the answer is easy: there is a huge change in cultural sensibility from modern to postmodern. Many Protestant churches, shaped by Christendom and modernity, tended to work well for moderns, but they do not work as well for postmoderns. The powerful current of modernity still flows, and it has been liberating and creative for the church in many ways. But it has also tended to result in a highly moral and highly institutional form of Christianity, not an especially spiritual one. People in modern, mainline Protestant churches became, says Graham Standish, "rational functionalists."[11] Modern Christians tended to explain mystery and miracle (that is, they often explained them away), and they proposed moral values as universal truth detached from religious experience and God. What was missing was the spiritual connection and experience, the experience of a numinous and transcendent, yet immanent and sacred Other. Thus it is no accident that during the last thirty years, while interest in spirituality has become huge, that interest has not always — or even often — translated into enthusiasm for the established churches. They have not been offering spirituality as much as morality and corporeality.

While Christendom meant that churches often forgot how to do transformation and formation, that is, they forgot how to let God form Christians because they assumed that everyone was already Christian, modernity has meant that churches actually grew suspicious of spiritu-

11. Graham Standish, *Becoming a Blessed Church* (Herndon, VA: Alban Institute, 2005), p. 15.

ality and of the truth claims of the faith. Churches and their leaders have tended to emphasize "rational religion" and morality (religion drained of spiritual experience), and have thus adapted to the cultural context of American Christendom and responded to the modern era. My point is not that this was bad or good. I believe that, in many ways, the Protestant and mainstream churches did a pretty good job in the modern era and Christendom culture. My point is that we don't live there anymore. And my further point is that these matters are not about you who have been members of the modern, established, mainline church. They are not the fault of your church, your pastor, or your denomination. They are just the way it is. It's not about you. Except that it also *is* about you — but that's the next chapter.

However, before we move on to how it *is* about you and about me, let me underscore a crucial point. In order to respond and take action, congregations and their leaders need to first get a handle on what's going on. We need to define reality correctly and as accurately as possible. Moreover, we need to help one another understand not only how it is, but that it is not about us in the sense of blame or failure. It is crucial to understand Christendom and its implications, how it is no longer the sea we swim in, and to understand the powerful current of modernity, which is no longer as powerful as it once was.

"What, then, shall we do?" asked those who heard Peter on the day of Pentecost. It all began with Peter reframing their experience, giving them new interpretive lenses, and telling them that the way they had been putting things together and explaining them was not accurate or helpful. As Peter enumerated what God had been up to in their history and in the crucifixion and resurrection of Jesus, he was saying, "This is what's really going on!" In the Acts story of the early church, the real issue is not moral failure, but ignorance. Peter says that the people were ignorant, and he set about bringing illumination and a better definition of the situation in order to overcome ignorance. In some respects, we in the mainline churches have also been ignorant of, or at least not fully cognizant of, the big picture that I have tried to portray in this chapter.

That's the place to start. What do we do next? We describe reality as accurately as we possibly can. Then we can begin to talk about how we are to respond. And then we can move on to how this sea change *is* about us and how we need to respond to it.

For Reflection and Discussion

- Imagine a spectrum with "modern" at one end and "postmodern" at the other. Where would you locate yourself on that spectrum and why?
- Assess the balance of "head" (or reason) and "heart" (or emotion) in your congregation. Would you say that one predominates, or are they fairly evenly balanced?

And Yet . . . It *Is* About You

If it's true that "it's not about you," that is, that the challenges facing congregations as the twenty-first century begins are owing to large cultural and religious shifts in North American culture, the next important conversation may come as a surprise: "And yet . . . it *is* about you." It is about you and me, and about the community of us together in our congregations. It is about how we respond to shifts in culture and religion in our time. At an earlier moment in the Christian church, another sea change in the church's story — Pentecost — two questions frame the events of that watershed. When the crowds of Passover pilgrims in Jerusalem witnessed the outpouring of the Spirit on the day of Pentecost, they asked: "What does this mean?" One might put that initial query slightly differently: "What's going on?"

We can begin by more accurately describing reality, describing what is going on. The sea change in religion in North America and the challenges facing all churches, especially the mainline Protestant congregations, are not something you made happen by action or neglect, nor are they peculiar to your congregation or denomination. They are, in Diana Butler Bass's words, "just the way it is." If you are a pastor, the end of Christendom wasn't brought on by the sermon you preached last Sunday or last year, or by the fact that your personality has too little (or too much) sparkle. If you are a dedicated layperson, the fact that things have changed and the church is not the way you remember it being forty years ago isn't because you are not as smart or as good or as Christian as your parents or grandparents were. It's not about you.

Yet the way forward *is* about you and about us in the sense that it has everything to do with how we respond to the sea change and to the shifting currents of a postmodern world. Because how we *respond* to the shifts and challenges I described in the preceding chapter is up to us. There was a second key question the early believers asked on Pentecost. After Peter had responded to the first question ("What does this mean?") with his sermon (Acts 2:14-36), those who heard him preach asked the second question that frames Pentecost: "What, then, shall we do?" (Acts 2:37) Note well these two important questions. In the first conversation I attempted to explore the "What does this mean?" question. Now I want to turn to the second question that the crowd asked Peter: "What, then, shall we do?" implies that it *is* about us!

Human Beings as Answerers

The mid-twentieth-century theologian H. Richard Niebuhr, the younger of the famous brothers, said that a scripturally shaped understanding of the nature of human beings is that human beings are answerers. "What is implicit in the idea of responsibility is the image of man-the-answerer, man engaged in dialogue, man acting in response to action upon him."[1] Rabbi Abraham Heschel, Niebuhr's contemporary, is said to have offered a similar insight: "Religion begins with an awareness that something is being asked of us." No one pastor, church, or denomination has been responsible for creating the sea change, but it is a phenomenon that brings real opportunities as well as dangers. Something is being asked of us. It is up to us how we shall respond and thus how we shall answer the God who is at work in the midst of these enormous changes.

At an earlier time and juncture in the story of faith, Israel's exile during the sixth century BCE, the prophet Ezekiel challenged the resignation of his people in the face of the exilic sea change. He reminded them of their capacity to answer and told them that there were no more excuses and that something was being asked of them in this new and difficult time. "What do you mean," asked the prophet, "by repeating this proverb concerning the land of Israel, 'The parents have eaten sour grapes,

---

1. H. Richard Niebuhr, *The Responsible Self* (New York: Harper and Row, 1963), p. 56.

and the children's teeth are set on edge'? As I live, says the Lord God, this proverb shall no more be used by you in Israel. Know that all lives are mine; the life of the parent as well as the life of the child is mine: it is only the person who sins that shall die" (Ezek. 18:2-4). The prophet's hearers, in the midst of their exile, had come to believe that their situation was the result of the sinful choices of previous generations: their parents and ancestors had eaten sour grapes. Furthermore, there was nothing that they, a subsequent generation, could do about it but live with the consequences. Ezekiel challenged that view of things, its implicit passivity and timidity. No, said the prophet, even in exile we retain some measure of freedom. We must exercise our ability to respond.

The theological point is also a psychological truism: we seldom have complete control over what life brings, but it *is* up to us how we respond to it. Perhaps we can hunker down and hope that all this will eventually blow over. Not from Ezekiel's point of view. He urged God's people to rise to the occasion by trying to understand what was required of them at their moment in history. We may choose to angrily vent our frustrations on one other, or blame others, because the world we knew well has collapsed. Or we may bring our grief and lamentations before God, who is capable of transforming loss and lament into hope and praise.

We find further clues and hints for our time in the Pentecost story. On the day of Pentecost (Acts 2), Peter began his sermon by taking a familiar text from the prophet Joel for a familiar occasion, Pentecost. Peter reframed both of them, the text and the occasion, in such a way as to redescribe the world and show what was really going on. By that time, Jews were expecting a day of national celebration and self-congratulation when they gathered in Jerusalem for Pentecost. Pentecost was not all that different from our own 4th of July in its more self-congratulatory forms. But Peter redescribed their world. Instead of portraying their situation as Joel was often read, as a world where God was on the side of his people, the Jews, and everyone else could expect God's judgment, Peter claimed that God had done and was doing a new thing. He argued that many of God's people and most of their institutions had missed what God was doing and urgently needed to come to a different way of construing reality. It wasn't the Romans or Samaritans or Ninevites who needed to repent, said Peter: "It's us." Or as the old spiritual puts it, "Not the preacher, not the teacher, but it's me, O Lord, standing in the need of prayer." It's me . . .

it's us, said Peter. Surely Peter understood who and where he was, and he shared in this call to repentance, considering his own strenuous denials of Jesus and his failure when the chips were down.

Just as first-century official and institutional Judaism had missed and misinterpreted what God was up to during Jesus' time, I wonder whether many of us mainline and established Christians have not also missed what God is up to in our time. As we anxiously monitor our losses and watch the bottom line, as we complain about the Religious Right or the megachurches and self-righteously claim that we are the true-blue and truly enlightened, have we missed or misinterpreted what God is doing as Christendom and modernity decline and a new world emerges? Rather than smugly assuring ourselves of our virtue and only pointing out the need for others to wake up and turn around, perhaps we, too, are ripe for hearing the world redescribed (as I attempted in the preceding chapter) as well as hearing God's call to wake up and turn around. "What, then, shall we do?" asked those who heard Peter's sermon on Pentecost. "Repent," answered Peter. "Wake up, do a 180, and answer with as much grace and courage as you can muster."

This is the focus of this chapter — really of the rest of the book. It is about you and about me. Building on the preceding conversation, this second one is about how we answer God in our own time and in our congregations. Rather than denying or bemoaning the sea change, can we discern God's Spirit at work and respond by changing the conversation in directions that encourage faithful response? One challenge that faces those who want to change the conversation is what might be considered stuck or nonproductive conversations. Such conversations tend to reinforce a picture of reality, of "what is going on," that is either inaccurate or self-serving or both. Stuck conversations go round and round and end up pretty much where they began, and in doing so they encourage the sense of resignation and passivity that Ezekiel was assaulting. In his book *The Fifth Discipline: The Art and Practice of the Learning Organization*, Peter Senge refers to these stuck conversations as "learning disabilities." It is not only individuals who experience learning disabilities; organizations and congregations have learning disabilities as well.[2] In the next part of this conversation I will touch on some of the typical stuck con-

2. Peter Senge, *The Fifth Discipline: The Art and Practice of the Learning Organization* (New York: Doubleday, 1990), pp. 18ff.

versations that snare congregations. Following this look at stuck conversations, I will describe a distinction drawn from the work of leadership teacher Ronald Heifetz that is critical to making our conversations more productive: his seminal distinction between "technical problems" and "adaptive challenges." Later in the book, in Conversation 6, I shall again make use of the concept of adaptive challenges to show how this tool is helpful in moving beyond many stuck conversations.

A crucial step in moving away from stuck conversations and engaging in the adaptive work before us is to acknowledge grief. Sometimes our stuck conversations are a way of protecting ourselves against the grief and loss that is part of the sea change we have identified. Until we name and experience the grief, we are unlikely to be able to move on to more productive conversations and to hopeful, engaged responses. Therefore, I will spend some time in the next section of this chapter on our grief work. The concluding portion of this second conversation is about building a sense of urgency. Individual people, as well as congregations, are unlikely to engage in important adaptive work unless they have some sense that "this is important," a sense that "we have to get on this right now." How can leaders and participants in congregations stir a sense of urgency? All of these are elements of this second conversation: our capacity to respond as answerers, naming some typical stuck conversations, facing our grief, distinguishing between technical and adaptive work, and building a sense of urgency. If we are going to change the conversation that is going on in our congregations, we must begin to embrace and hold in tension both of these statements: "It's not about you," "and yet . . . it *is* about you." This is not an either/or choice; it is a both/and realization.

For Reflection and Discussion
- Reflect on or talk about an experience when you, or someone you know, "rose to the occasion" or "answered" life's changes and challenges with courage and grace.

Stuck Conversations

In my work as a pastor, teacher, and congregational consultant, I have noticed four conversations occurring in congregations that go no-

where. Indeed, neither the conversations nor the congregations go anywhere. They are stuck. I'm sure there are a few more stuck conversations that your congregation can think of to add to these four, but these
are sufficient to illustrate the phenomenon. These four conversations,
or patterns of response to our new situation, are neither helpful or
faithful. In fact, they are genuinely counterproductive. They include:
(1) Blame Games, (2) "We're Not Like Them," (3) "Where's the Silver
Bullet?" and (4) "If Only. . . ."

But before we take a brief look at each of those four stuck conversations, one of the reasons that these stuck conversations ("learning disabilities," in Senge's formulation) can be so powerful and frustrating is
that too many churches have been successful in turning their congregations into clubs. Such congregations become gatherings for those who
have been around and been together for a long time. When I visited one
declining congregation, I parked my car on a side street ten minutes before the service and went to the front door of the church. It was closed
— not only closed, but locked! I walked completely around the building
until I came to the back door, where I entered the church and encoun-
tered a longtime member whom I knew.

"Sally," I said, "the front door, it's not open, it's locked."

"We all know to come in the back door," said Sally, who had been a
member of the congregation for nearly fifty years. This was a church
that, in theory at least, hoped to attract new members!

When a church turns into a club, something else happens: our conversations become predictable and self-reinforcing. They are not leav-
ened by the perceptions of the stranger or the newcomer. When a
church loses its capacity to welcome the stranger, to practice genuine
hospitality, sometimes it is God whom we have shut out. Many times in
Scripture, God — or one or more of God's messengers — come to the
faithful in the form of a stranger or in some disguise. When the church
becomes a club where "we all know to come in the back door," then it is
much more likely that our conversations will be stuck in the "same old,
same old." One way to counteract this, besides working at hospitality
and encouraging strangers to share their gifts with us, is to get out and
visit other churches. Take a group on a field trip to another church and
see how it goes about its task. This will freshen your conversation. Or
intentionally bring in an outsider in the form of a guest teacher or consultant. Ask that person, after she or he has spent some time in your

midst, to give you a frank assessment. Both are ways of introducing something fresh into conversations that turn stale when churches turn into clubs, lifestyle enclaves, or gated communities.

The blame game is a very common form of stuck conversation. Sometimes congregations blame their leaders: "We just haven't been able to get the right pastor, not since wonderful Dr. Lewis was with us." "If only we could get the right minister, everything would be okay again." Leadership is important, even critical, but leaders never do it by themselves, and we seldom can move into the future by attempting to reproduce the past. A variation on the theme is that clergy blame their congregations: "This is a congregation that just doesn't get it," mumble the clergy. "No one here really wants to change. They would rather die than change." Again, there may be some truth in such laments, but when we ministers find ourselves blaming our congregations, it is usually time to take a good hard look at ourselves. Too many relationships between clergy and congregation fall into the same trap and pattern as unhealthy, unhappy marriages. We blame our partners: "If only she would change." "If only he wasn't such a numbskull." Again, there's probably some truth there, but in good marriage counseling we usually give up on waiting for our spouse to get fixed and start dealing with our own needs and issues. Other popular forms of the blame game are to blame the denomination or the judicatory or their key staff people, or to blame some segment of the congregation, such as "the old people" or "the young people" or the choir or [fill-in-the-blank]. Finally, people in congregations may choose to blame the wider community: "People here just don't care about church, or each other, or their children or [fill-in-the-blank]." While having someone to blame may provide temporary psychological satisfaction and relief, it seldom contributes to positive growth and change.

A second stuck conversation that has become common, as mainline churches have perceived the springing up and growth of new and more conservative congregations, is to put a lot of energy into *defining your church against those "others":*

"We're not like those conservatives . . . or 'evangelicals' or 'fundamentalists.'"

"Who are you then?"

"Well, we're not like them!" In politics, the Democratic Party has done this for some years: it has seemed to let the Republican Party set the agenda and then has said, "We're not like them." Again, there's some truth — and even some value — in this kind of self-identification. Some conservative congregations seem to be more focused on personal salvation and moral certainty than are many mainline congregations. Saying "we're different from what you may have experienced in the past" is fine as long as saying "we're not like them" isn't the only thing we have to say for ourselves. We may thus have our own version of the self-righteous judgment of the Pharisee who, while praying in the temple, glanced over at the tax collector and said, "I thank you, God, that I am not like other people, and in particular not like that tax collector there!" (Luke 18:11).

Conversations in congregations become stuck when they boil down to defining ourselves over against the megachurch down the road, or the fundamentalists on television, or the politicos of the Religious Right. We may offer critique and self-differentiation, but not arrogantly or defensively. It is much more important for us to have productive conversations that will turn to who God is calling us to be and how God is at work in our lives and life together. The name Protestant does not mean perpetual protest, always being against someone else. The word "Protestant" comes from *pro-* ("for") and *testari* ("to testify"). What are we for? What testimony do we offer about God and about God's work in our midst?

The search for the silver bullet, a third stuck conversation, is ubiquitous and is in some ways the flip side of the blame-game conversation. The silver bullet is the agent that will kill the enemy or magically solve our problems: it may be the perfect pastor, a better building or new church home, the right youth program or youth director, having more money, even changing denominations, or [fill-in-the-blank]. More often than not, the problem is not "out there," not external to us. It is internal to us. Usually a change in our hearts and our minds is required. It is developing a capacity to work with the pastoral leadership that God has provided rather than folding our arms on our chests and sitting back to wait for the right pastor to arrive. It may be learning to make the best use of the facilities we have rather than lamenting that those facilities are not as good as the nearby Methodist or Assembly of God churches. Great youth directors are wonderful indeed, but great youth directors are usually an expression of partnership between parents, youths, and members of a congregation who care about and are willing to work to make a great youth ministry happen. Long ago, when the children of Israel were looking for the silver bullet, Moses reminded them that they need not ask, "Who will go up to heaven for us?" or "Who will cross the sea and get it?" "No," said Moses, "the word is very near to you; it is in your mouth and in your heart that you may hear it and do it" (Deut. 30:12-14).

A variation on the silver bullet conversation (and still a stuck conversation) that is frequent enough to single out goes like this: "If only we could get twenty (or fifty or a hundred) new members, then we could make our budget and everything would be fine!" The next line usually goes: "So, Pastor (or staff, or evangelism committee), your job is to bring in those new members." Over the years, I have also seen a fair number of single adults in my office whose lament would go something like this: "Why don't I have anybody?" "Why can't I seem to find a relationship?" "Why am I not married?" I am sympathetic to that lament. Not finding a partner when you truly desire one is tough and disappointing, and it hurts. Yet I have noticed that, as long as those complaining of the need for another person to complete them or to fill their emptiness continue to sing that lament, the chances of their actually finding someone or being found by someone are slim. As soon as such people decide to get on with their life, to do the work they want to do and have energy for, to take up activities that look appealing or exciting to them, or to pay attention to their own health or challenges — then often someone seems to come along.

Congregations sometimes have the same sense that the individuals in the above example have: that new and perfect additions will make the difference in their lives. As long as we approach others — potential church members, for example — on the basis that they may be able to fill the empty place in us, it is unlikely to happen. When we face up to our own internal situation and turn to God to help us get on with the changes we need to make, amazingly, we seem much more interesting and attractive to others. When life and vitality are happening in a church, when people are excited to be there and are engaged in genuine spiritual growth, it tends to be contagious. If, on the other hand, not much is going on and we are looking for a bunch of new members to fill us up, chances are good that we will wait a very long time for that to happen. The refrain "if we can only get X number of new members to make the budget and fill the pews, then everything will be okay" is the basis of a stuck conversation.

There are other patterns of conversation that are stuck and not productive, conversations that cycle the same diagnoses and the same prescriptions over and over but go nowhere. We may be able to change that conversation by allowing newcomers and outsiders (such as a new pastor, for example) to say something we may not wish to hear, or by visiting other congregations for a fresh look at our own church, or by engaging a teacher or consultant from the outside to help us freshen up the conversation. I have found a useful tool for this work to be a distinction that is fundamental to the work of leadership teacher Ronald Heifetz.[3] As a tool for changing the conversation, let's consider his terms "technical problems" and "adaptive challenges" and the distinction between them.

For Reflection and Discussion

- Of the four "stuck conversations," which one have you heard in your congregation most often?
- In addition to these four, is there another stuck conversation that you think is important to name and discuss?

Technical Problems and Adaptive Challenges

As I have worked with congregations and denominations in recent years, I have found this distinction to be a very helpful analytical tool as well as a way of unhooking us from some of the more unproductive or stuck conversations above. By way of introduction, however, I think that it is important to point out that this distinction between technical problems and adaptive challenges, like many such educational devices, is cleaner and clearer in theory than it is in practice. In practice, technical and adaptive work often comes bundled, or, to put it in a slightly different way, many challenges have both technical and adaptive aspects. Still, the distinction is useful, indeed, more than useful — it is powerful. Beyond that, it helps define work that is intrinsically spiritual in nature. I shall return to that last point shortly. For now, it is important to concisely define and describe the distinction.

3. Ronald Heifetz, *Leadership without Easy Answers* (Cambridge, MA: Belknap Press, 1994), p. 35.

"Technical problems" are problems that are knowable and clearly described and named. If the church roof is leaking or we don't have sufficient space for all the children in the nursery, those are problems that are clear and known. Likewise, the solutions to technical problems are clear and known: they involve the application of existing technique. The church needs a new roof, or at least part of it needs to be repaired. We need another room for the nursery that is larger, or we need to expand the nursery into two rooms. The critical third characteristic of technical work is when we come to the question "Who does the work?" By and large, the answer to that question is: "experts and authorities." The roof problem will be dealt with by the trustees or the building committee, and they will hire a roofing contractor. The nursery issue will be addressed by the Sunday school superintendent, the Christian education board, and perhaps the building committee. Perhaps a contractor, maybe even an architect, will be involved. In some measure, all of these groups and individuals are experts and authorities who are given the responsibility of dealing with a particular technical problem.

Adaptive challenges are different. And in these cases, even naming the challenge entails learning and change. We may not know — or may not accurately know — the nature of the challenge we are facing. For many years the mainline Protestant denominations and congregations have named their problem in a technical way. They called it "membership decline," and they knew the solution: "membership growth techniques" or "evangelism." And who did the work? Experts and authorities: that is, pastors, church growth or membership committees, denominational specialists, and the like. Except that it hasn't worked. It has not worked because we have been dealing with it as if it were a clear and known technical problem, a problem that could be called "membership decline." But we are dealing with larger, more complex matters: we are dealing with an adaptive challenge of the sea-change variety that I spoke of in the preceding chapter.

Christendom has ended, and thus the ways that we have learned to do and to be church that worked in that time are no longer so useful. Sometimes the known ways are counterproductive. *Learning* about the church in Christendom and today, and *change*, new and alternative ways of doing church, are required. Not only are learning and change a part of naming the challenge when it is adaptive work we face; but identifying or discovering good responses to the challenges we face also means learning and change. We don't know, at least not as easily or as precisely as we might in a technical problem situation, what the appropriate response is to the more complex challenges. It is not simply a matter of applying existing and known techniques to solve a problem. There may well be more than one response.

Discovering what good responses are may mean moving beyond the techniques, strategies, and concepts we already know and have at our disposal to learn new ones. Finally, and this is crucial, who does the work when it is an adaptive challenge with which we are dealing? Not experts or authorities. They may have some role, but in the end the work must be done by those who have the problem, those who are facing the challenge. In other words, we cannot offload responsibility for learning to be the church in new ways in our new time onto clergy or seminaries or lay leaders or denominational staffs. This adaptive work requires the engagement of the church, of congregations, of all God's people.

Because our society has proven so efficient and capable in developing technical solutions, something for which we can be grateful and of which we may be proud, we have a tendency to imagine that everything is a technical problem that can be solved if only we find the right experts or authorities. Not true. There are many challenges we face that cannot be addressed this way. Medical care provides one example. Often medical problems are and can be approached as technical problems. For example, a person has heart disease, so we consult an expert, a coronary-care physician, and she prescribes a treatment plan. "Well, let's see," says the doctor, "we can try this combination of medications, or we can go with surgery." But then she continues: "Either way, you [the patient] will need to make some changes in your life. You'll need to exercise more, reduce your stress at work, and change your diet." In other words, not all the work can be done by an expert or authority. Some of the work, the adaptive work, will need to be shouldered by the patient. In the larger frame of medical practice, there are many new medications for different conditions and illnesses, a valid technical response for which we can, in most respects, be grateful. At the same time, however, we can also see that the costs of such a system are enormous. If they are not to undo us, we will need to do better, as we live longer, at preventive healthcare. That usually means adaptive work that patients, their families, and communities have to do to make for health and well-being.

Examples of technical and adaptive work in congregations stare us in the face at every turn. One congregation with whom I recently worked had identified its problem: the rate of worship attendance, as a percentage of their membership, was quite low — 20 percent. In fact, in comparison to similar-sized congregations of their denomination in their region, they were between 10 percent and 20 percent lower than those other congregations. What to do? Note that the matter had been framed as a problem, and a clear and known one at that. "Our worship attendance as a percentage of membership is too low. We should be at 30 percent or better, not 20 percent." The problem was clear, and the solution was to apply a known and existing technique, that is, start a new contemporary worship service. They hoped that this would appeal to those who didn't care for the two existing services. They planned to schedule the new contemporary service at 11:00 a.m., concurrent with the second existing service. Finally, who would do the work? The worship committee and the pastoral and music staff — those were the experts and authorities.

It could be that this congregation had analyzed its situation correctly, and its plan might work just fine. But I wasn't convinced. I suggested that another way to look at things might be to wonder whether their worship attendance rate, a longstanding pattern of 20 percent of their membership, might suggest that they were a church where the culture of the congregation did not consider worship participation as normative or essential to Christian life and spiritual growth. "Add your new contemporary service, if you wish," I said (though I added that I thought they ran the risk of diminishing their attendance at the current 11:00 service, which was already only 50-60 percent full), "but the real challenge may be to change the culture of this congregation in ways that make spiritual growth and worship central to your life and identity." In saying this, I was trying to suggest the adaptive dimension of the challenge they faced. Moreover, I wanted to encourage them not to assign all the responsibility for working on the problem to a worship committee or the worship leaders, but to engage the congregation as a whole in this work of changing the culture of the congregation: to become more clearly focused on spiritual growth and to highlight regular worship participation as a key to reaching that goal.

As I have noted above, the technical and adaptive dimensions often come bundled. There are probably some technical adjustments and changes that a congregation like the one just mentioned could — and should — make. Perhaps their sanctuary needed to be modified to encourage a different style of worship with more involvement. However, if there was truth in my analysis that their culture as a congregation was not one that placed high value on regular worship participation, then they would discover that all the technical adjustments in the world would be to no real avail without deeper changes. Change involves change in hearts and minds, which is the nature of adaptive work. It involves new learning, perhaps about the nature of Christian worship: how to take part in it, what it is and what it isn't, and worship's relationship to Christian life and growth in faith. When we overlook or do not take seriously the adaptive dimension of challenges in our congregations in favor of technical solutions driven by experts, we seldom make lasting progress.

There is one more facet of the technical/adaptive distinction that is worth noting. Adaptive work, or "engaging adaptive challenges," to use Heifetz's language, is intrinsically spiritual work. It is spiritual work precisely because it is about changing lives, about changing and transforming human hearts, minds, and communities. This point can be deepened by returning to the threefold sequence of adaptive work: naming and framing the challenge, discovering and learning forms of response, and then engaging in and doing the work by the people who have the problem or challenge.

Often the first step, naming and framing adaptive work and challenges, not only means learning and change; it also means loss and heightened awareness. The world is not as we thought, and we are not as we thought. We have harbored illusions that God asks us to surrender. If loss and heightened awareness are a part of the experience at the first step ("Hmm, maybe we are not a congregation that really gives a priority to worship or to being in God's presence"), the second frame involves risk, letting go, and surrender. Learning new ways and behaviors, gaining knowledge, and engaging in new practices will probably require us to step out of our comfort zones of familiarity and security. That's never easy, but it is always where we grow in faith and where we encounter God. Finally, taking on the work and engaging in it together means exercising responsibility or agency (the capacity to make a difference). It means learning trust as we learn new practices and respond to a God who is forever doing a new thing! Loss, heightened awareness, risk, letting go, responsibility, agency, deepening trust — these are the basics and the building blocks of spiritual growth. If and when we construe all problems as technical and delegate the solutions to experts or professionals, we miss our chance to grow in Christ.

Don't get me wrong. There is a time and place for the technical approach. If the roof is leaking, the furnace doesn't work, or we need a good resource for adult Bible study, I am happy to have experts and professionals to call on. But many of the important challenges we face in congregations are not technical in nature; they are adaptive challenges that involve changed lives. Indeed, one might well argue that Jesus was seldom, if ever, in the business of technical problem-solving. He was forever creating or naming adaptive work and inviting people to changed lives. For example, in the story of the loaves and fishes in John 6, the crowd Jesus had fed the previous day was pursuing him. He told them bluntly: "You are looking for me because you ate your fill of the bread. Do not work for the food that perishes, but for the food that endures for eternal life" (John 6:26-27). The crowd wanted Jesus to be an expert or authority, a miracle worker who would fix their problem by producing a steady supply of bread. Instead, Jesus gave them a problem and the work: "Work for the food that endures for eternal life." The initial feeding was a sign, pointing beyond itself to God and to a dimension or quality of life that Jesus called "eternal." He invited, indeed challenged, the pursuing crowd to "see," which for John means to come to faith. Jesus was not after "oohs and aahs" in response to his deeds. He was after changed lives! "Do not work for the food that perishes, but for the food that endures for eternal life."

Heifetz's distinction between technical problems and adaptive challenges is, in my experience, something that people understand and find useful. It does allow us to move beyond stuck conversations, which often frame as technical problems what is really adaptive work. It helps us identify the work of new life that is our own. In this framework, grace may be understood as the power that God grants to those engaged in such adaptive work and its several dimensions of loss and awareness, risk and letting go, responsibility and agency. With this in mind, let's pay more extended attention to the element of grief work.

For Reflection and Discussion
- Identify a technical problem facing your congregation.
- Identify an adaptive challenge facing your congregation.

Grief Work to Be Done

In our personal lives, if there has been loss or disappointment, we are not usually really ready to take the next steps until we have grieved our loss. We may feel that it is time to begin a job search, to open ourselves to a new relationship, or to get on with some other important life challenge. But our readiness for any of these actions depends to a significant degree on our having processed the grief of losing a job where we had been secure, for example, or having a marriage or relationship end in death or divorce, or some other end-of-a-life chapter, such as the children leaving home.

I ran into a brick wall in my second pastoral call, a brick wall named depression. I hit that wall in part because I had not grieved the loss of my first congregation and that initial pastoral experience. My first pastorate had lasted four years, four very rich years for me, for my family, and for the congregation. I had discovered joy and competence as a minister. My family had made a home in the community; our second child was born there, and our first began school there. The congregation had taken on significant new mission programs as well as shouldering and completing a capital fund drive and building program. It had been a rich and special time for all of us. But I was a young-man-in-a-hurry, too soon responding to a new challenge at which I might prove myself.

We packed up and headed off to the next call, a congregation that really did have some very daunting challenges. After about a year at the new church, I found myself slumped at the foot of a figurative brick wall. Part of what landed me there was that I had not grieved my happy first pastorate and the known world it had become. I had not grieved that loss or let go of that first church sufficiently so that I was fully able to welcome a new congregation into my heart. In some ways, I even imagined that I was going off on a kind of mission trip and that I would return after a while. But that's not how these things work. For a pastor and family, leaving a congregation is a kind of death. Grief is important, and it won't be rushed or reduced to a program. It has its own time and season, and it is work that needs to be done.

There's a lot of grieving going on in many mainline Protestant congregations today, and it needs to go on. When we do not acknowledge our grief or believe grieving is not allowed, we tend to get bottled up and opt for answers that don't answer and fixes that don't fix. Therefore, before we go on to suggest helpful and faithful responses to the sea change and the fresh currents, it is important that we acknowledge our grief. And there is much to grieve. American Christendom, for all its limitations, was a good, ordered, reliable world: it was the world of the small towns and agrarian economies of my grandparents; the suburban villages of my parents; the world of the neighborhood church often closely connected to the neighborhood public school. It was Sunday school, church picnics, and ministers who were like fathers. It was confirmation classes as large as the junior-high graduating class and as sure as fall football. Several years before he died, my father gave me a small framed object resting on velvet cloth. It looked like a military medal, and it could have been, because he fought in World War II. But when I looked more closely, I discovered that he had given me his perfect attendance pins for six years of Sunday school at the Congregational Church of Enterprise, Oregon.

Not only was it a known world; this was a world where the people of the mainline Protestant churches had power, clout, and status. By and large, we don't have those assets to the same degree today. Old First Church may still be there downtown under the same name and banner, but when you look inside, you will not find the movers and shakers or a downtown elite. The pews are not quite as full as they once were, and in some places they may be nearly empty. The folks who find their places in the pews these days don't always look like society's strong and secure. Sometimes the crowd looks almost as old as Abraham and Sarah (to whom God, improbably, kept promising parenthood of not just one child but of a host of people as numerous as the grains of sand on the seashore). More often than not, the pastor in the pulpit is a woman.

That represents a lot of change. I am convinced that hidden in this new condition of the church are seeds of renewal, as well as new and rich opportunities. But before we can see them, we need to clear the ground and turn the soil. We need to acknowledge our grief for the world many of us knew and loved, one in which many of us had power and prominence.

Here's another little truth about that world: it was a world where white Anglo-Saxon Protestants (WASPs) were the social establishment. The racial, cultural, language, and religious group that peopled our mainline churches was the nation's de facto establishment. I do not mention this to induce guilt. WASPs in mainline churches and denominations have been treated to a pretty steady diet of guilt and self-recrimination in recent decades, with a mostly negative effect. We have been told, from many quarters, of our racism, sexism, nationalism, homophobia, consumption, and sinful affluence nearly ad nauseam. And then we've been expected to get up and change the world. Not surprisingly, it hasn't often worked. As one pastor said to me, "You can't keep telling people week after week that they are the problem and then expect them to have a lot of positive energy for making the world a better place." Too many of us mainline church leaders have made the mistake of kicking people when they are down. While the Religious Right has made another kind of mistake — stoking racial, cultural, class, and national resentments — the once mainline has often laid on the guilt in such thick layers that it is no wonder people have grown weary and dispirited.

We do well to remind ourselves of those oft-discussed symptoms and stages of grief that have become a staple of psychotherapy: denial, anger, guilt, bargaining, depression, and acceptance. Different congregations are in different places as they grieve the loss of the past and process these experiences. Some have pretty much done their grief work and moved on; they realize that the world they once knew is gone and will not come back. Others are stuck in denial, hoping that next year will turn out to be 1959 instead of 2009. In a good many congregations, unacknowledged and unprocessed grief comes out in anger and blame; though they are fueled by genuine emotions, seldom are these helpful responses. Furthermore, grief that is not acknowledged or experienced blocks our awareness of God in the present and saps our hope for the future.

For Reflection and Discussion
- What are some indications, where you live or work, that the predominance of white Anglo-Saxon Protestants is a thing of the past?
- What feelings do you experience about these changes?

Developing a Sense of Urgency

The sea changes in North American society and religion often give rise to anxiety, which is understandable. Anxiety, if it does not become overwhelming, may be a useful catalyst for response. But anxiety can easily overwhelm us, and when it does, our responses are driven and reactive. A sense of urgency is preferable to anxiety. Urgency means that the work before us is compelling and important; moreover, it has high priority: "We need to get on this right now. It can't wait." How can congregational leaders foster or develop a necessary sense of urgency about responding to the challenges of our changed world and our new time? How can this conversation, "It *is* about you," be furthered by a sense of urgency, excitement, and hope? The final portion of this chapter engages these questions by proposing some strategies for encouraging a sense of urgency. Leadership teacher John Kotter argues that developing a sense of urgency is crucial if organizations and communities, including congregations and denominations, are to change in productive and faithful ways.[4] Without a sense of urgency, adaptive work is not likely to happen. How, then, do congregational leaders go about building that sense of urgency? What follows are six strategies for building a sense of urgency.

Describing our situation. Before prescribing what to do, good leaders describe what is going on. Our first conversation about the demise of Christendom and the waning of modernity was just such a describing — or redescribing — of our situation in North America, particularly among mainline Protestant congregations. There is no need to repeat that analysis here, but I can highlight some of its implications. During American Christendom, mainline Protestant congregations tended to have a guaranteed "market share," and our share of the market was a majority share. Today this is much less true. Our market share has diminished between 40 percent and 70 percent for mainline denominations in the last forty years. Moreover, people do not necessarily show up at our churches simply because their parents or grandparents did or because they live nearby. Second, there are plausible and visible alternatives to our mainline Protestant congregations. Thirty years ago no one had ever heard of a megachurch; today every town and city has one or more of the big-box church types. Furthermore, while religion in the era of American Christendom tended to mean "Protestant, Catholic, or Jew," today there are as many options on the menu of spirituality as there are channels on television.

---

4. John Kotter, *Leading Change* (Cambridge, MA: Harvard Business School Press, 1996), pp. 35-49.

A third characteristic of our new situation is that we cannot depend on the culture or our society to do Christian formation for us. People in North America no longer learn the stories of the Bible by growing up here. Children do not learn Christmas carols or the Christmas story at their public schools. Almost no one has taught young people, or even adults, how to pray, how to practice discernment, or how to read or study Scripture. Congregations that assume people come with these things simply by virtue of growing up in North America will be mistaken. Another implication of our new time, particularly its postmodern aspect, is that there is a new interest in and openness to spirituality. No longer is reason king. Other forms of human knowing, other kinds of human experience, including whatever we mean by "spiritual," are taken seriously. These are just some of the realities of our new situation. Describing them and providing information about them can help to build a sense of urgency.

In describing our situation, congregational leaders may and should also provide information about their particular congregation and community. Some congregations may think that matters such as membership and attendance are pretty much what they have always been. That is what one new pastor with whom I worked was told. But when she looked at the numbers over a thirty-year period, she could read a different story, a story of slow but steady decline. To offer a different example, I recall the year our congregation took something like a "time and talent" survey: we asked members to indicate their interest in a variety of church activities, including "serving on a church board" (with the boards listed) and "being part of a ministry team" (with a list of current ministry teams). Forty-seven people expressed interest in serving on a board (there were 125 board positions in all), while more than 700 indicated interest in one or another "ministry team." Reporting this information helped to build a sense of urgency for supporting the development of ministry teams and restructuring the congregation in ways that required fewer persons to serve on standing boards.

Letting people feel the pinch of reality, says Ron Heifetz, is a somewhat different way to describe the situation and to help leaders who are trying to engage people in adaptive work.[5] This means that, instead of do-

---

5. Ronald Heifetz and Donald L. Laurie, "The Work of Leadership," in *Harvard Business Review on Point* (Cambridge, MA: Harvard Business School Press, 2002), p. 9.

ing what they often do, that is, protect those they lead from reality, leaders who want to encourage a sense of urgency will let people encounter some hard truths about the reality of the situation. A business CEO may tell his board about new competitors or the loss of market share. A pastor, like the one I mentioned above, may report that things are not as they have always been, but have been on a slow but steady decline. The business of letting people feel the pinch of reality is important, but it needs to be used in moderate doses so that a congregation will not become discouraged. Tell the truth, as Paul said, but tell the truth in love.

Another way to let people feel the pinch of reality is to encourage groups to make field trips to other congregations that are creative and vital. The point is not to become imitators of that other congregation's style or techniques; it is simply to see that there is a varied world out there and that there are different ways to do church. Many who faithfully attend their own congregations, a practice for which we can be grateful, may not have much awareness of other styles, options, and forms, nor, for that matter, of the ferment in North American religious and spiritual life today. Gaining an awareness of that via firsthand experience can help people feel the pinch of reality and develop their own sense of urgency.

Empowering leadership from below or from the outside is a third way of building a sense of urgency. In many long-established, stable, or declining congregations, those in leadership have been in those positions for a long time. Newcomers tend to be in the minority if they are in leadership at all, and thus they may not feel free to speak up and share their perceptions. How can those who might provide leadership, but who are not in the established core, be heard? Pastors and other influential persons in the congregation will need to make it a priority to empower those who, by virtue of relative newness, youth, or different social-economic-racial characteristics from the majority, are not getting heard or taken seriously. There are many ways to go about this, from surveys to intentional board nominations to gathering ad hoc and think-tank groups to creating settings in which it is safe for those who are not on the inside to speak. One tool or technique that may be especially useful is called "Max-Mix." That means creating groups at congregational meetings, forums, and retreats where there is a maximum of mixing among young and old, new and longtime members, people of different views and experiences. When people hear only the views of those closest to them, as often happens, a congregation's capacity to gain a new sense of urgency or energy is diminished. "Max-Mix" experiences stir the pot and fuel the conversation. As new voices are heard and a congregation's base of experience is broadened and deepened, a congregation can develop a sense of urgency.

Appreciative inquiry is a fourth strategy for building urgency, one that can hold in balance the practice of empowering leadership from below or the outside. It is an approach that draws attention to what a congregation is currently doing well. Some of the best chapters in a congregation's life and history can be built on in the present. If we emphasize only the pinch of reality or the perspectives of newcomers, we risk missing the good ongoing work, and that may create a sense of discouragement or defensiveness in a congregation. Appreciative inquiry means that we focus not only on where there are problems or where we can improve, but also on where things have gone well and are still going well. Where are lives being touched, cared for, and changed in our congregation? That kind of good ministry is going on in every church. Support it and then build on it. In one situation, while doing some research into a congregation's past, I discovered that it had had a great track record of starting new congregations fifty years earlier. Remembering this story helped that congregation build a sense of urgency for starting another new church in a new time.

Changing the story we tell about ourselves is a fifth way to develop a congregation's sense of urgency and excitement. Sometimes the narrative we have about ourselves is not a very exciting or interesting one: "Oh, we're Old First, been there forever." Though Old First may be a venerable church, there's nothing particularly inviting or energizing about such a story. In many of our congregations and denominations the story we have been telling about ourselves for some time now is a narrative of decline. And then we're surprised we don't have a lot of visitors or new members! In my own denomination, the United Church of Christ, the story we told about ourselves for twenty-five years was just such a "narrative of decline." Then, early in the new century, we launched something we called the "God is Still Speaking Initiative": it included television commercials, new websites, banners, and much more. A key symbol of that initiative is a comma, which was drawn from the statement "Never put a period where God has placed a comma." Gradually we learned to tell a new story about ourselves: "We're the church of 'God is Still Speaking'" and "we're the church of the comma." What had been a negative self-image and story became a positive one, and this helped us build a new sense of urgency and excitement.

Finally, and perhaps most important of all, urgency comes from *the gospel itself, the belief in our message and community.* To a significant degree, long-established, mainline congregations have lost a sense of a good "evangelical urgency," a passion about the Good News. This I will investigate at greater length as part of the next conversation, "A New Heart." But if we don't believe that the gospel message is true and meaningful, and if we don't believe that our congregation is a place where people can meet and be met by the living God, then we are unlikely to have much of a sense of urgency. Urgency flows from the belief and experience of the church's faith and life as loving, life-giving, healing, and full of hope. For some conservative Christians, evangelical urgency is drawn from the belief that personal salvation and life beyond the grave is only for Christians. Many mainline Protestants do not see it that way: they are more concerned about living a Christian life here and now than they are about where they will be after they die. In my view, this is as it should be. But we need to become more urgent and passionate about life-before-death. Many people out there long for a meaningful spiritual life, for a connection with God, and for a community of authentic people who are making a difference. Mainline Protestant congregations can be all of those things, because what we do and what we are matters. It matters enormously! And that is the real and the best source of urgency.

For Reflection and Discussion
- Of these six ideas for developing a sense of urgency, which seems most urgent to you for your situation?
- Why do you love your church? Articulate a reason that's real for you.
- How could you share that with someone who could become interested in your church?

A Concluding Word

It *is* about you, and me, and us together. God has brought us to a new time. There are things we miss about the earlier era of American Christendom. There are parts of that experience that are precious and that we must carry forward into a new time; but there are also things that are expendable, things that have become excess baggage. Sorting out what is precious from what is expendable is part of the important work that is before us, and we shall turn to that in upcoming conversations. Some of the ways we have been church and have done church in the past no longer fit this new time, and this new time can liberate us from some behaviors and experiences that are best left behind. God has not brought us this far to leave us now. God will be with us in this new time.

A New Heart

Not long ago I was working with the congregations of a particular ju-dicatory that had developed a fourfold plan for growth and develop-ment. One of their four priorities was "Renewing Our Faith." My host and the event organizers confessed that, of their four priorities, that one seemed to be the most difficult for them to get hold of, and to make progress on. I observed that "renewing faith" implies that we already have it and that we only need to dust it off or heat it up. Per-haps, I continued, we might do better to think less in terms of "re-newing" and more in terms of "newing," or, to use Marcus Borg's for-mulation, "meeting Jesus (again) for the first time."[1] The civic faith that was operative in many of our congregations for so many years was a compound of good citizenship, personal moral virtues, and do-ing what we could to make the world a better place. Of course, there's nothing wrong with that; it's just that there's nothing specifi-cally Christian about it. Merely renewing civic faith will not get us headed in the right direction. Something more — something deeper — is required.

I do not say this theoretically, but from my own experience. Raised within a civic-faith church that was wonderful in many ways, I never-theless found myself ill prepared, that is, not adequately formed as a person of faith, for ordained ministry. I had learned something about

1. Marcus Borg, *Meeting Jesus (Again) for the First Time* (San Francisco: Harper, 1994).

the Bible and about theology in seminary, to be sure, but not nearly enough. I had not learned anything there about spiritual practices. And I found that ministry was truly impossible without them. In other words, I found that the civic faith of my youth and culture was insufficient. I had to go deeper. I had to surrender my illusions of control and self-sufficiency and learn to let God be God for me. I had to get a new heart.

When the Jerusalem crowd asked Peter their famous second question in Acts 2, "What, then, shall we do?" Peter answered without hesitation: "Repent and be baptized, every one of you, in the name of Jesus Christ so that your sins may be forgiven; and you will receive the gift of the Holy Spirit" (Acts 2:37-38). We sometimes construe "repentance" as simply meaning personal remorse, but that's too narrow. It means something more and something better. It means "turning around," facing and moving in a new and different direction. One of the difficulties of civic faith is that it allows us, and in a way encourages us, to think of ourselves as "the good people," those whose task is to do for others. This blinds us to our own need for repentance, our own need to get a new heart. If we are to change the conversation in our churches, we will not lose our emphasis on helping those in need, but we will perceive and confess our own need.

Peter's words define our need: "repentance" = turning around, a new direction; "baptism" = entry into the new community of promise created by God's act in Jesus Christ; "forgiven" = grace and mercy for our sins and brokenness; "gift of the Holy Spirit" = power for those resolved toward new lives and new communities of honesty, care, justice, and generosity.

In order for congregations of the once mainline churches to make progress and be vital in our new time, the word of "repentance" must be addressed *to us* as well, not as a scolding but as an invitation to a new heart. What follows in this conversation about "a new heart" is a fourfold focus on: (1) a living God and the God message; (2) the power and purpose of Scripture; (3) evangelism, from "them" to "us"; and (4) theology, from professional to amateur. The reader may respond, "Great, but how do we do these things?" I suggest some directions in this chapter, and I address "Christian formation" as an adaptive challenge in a subsequent chapter. But the "how" is also something you will discover in the ongoing conversation that is the life of your congregation.

For Reflection and Discussion
- What would be your hunch about why the group of congregations mentioned above found their priority of "renewing faith" to be difficult to accomplish?
- When you hear the word "repentance," what comes to mind? Do my comments suggest something different to you?

A Living God and the God Message

In Anne Tyler's novel *Saint Maybe,* nineteen-year-old Ian tells his parents, Doug and Bee Bedloe, of his decision to leave college and become an apprentice cabinetmaker to enable him to raise the young children of his deceased brother, Danny, and his sister-in-law, Lucy. Ian has arrived at this decision because of the influence in his life of Rev. Emmett and the Church of the Second Chance, a congregation that believes in actual atonement, that is, that you must do something "real" to be forgiven for your sins. Ian's sin was that he led his drunken brother to believe that his wife was unfaithful, after which Danny committed suicide by driving his car into a brick wall.

In the crucial scene in which Ian tells his parents of the change in the course of his life, church and faith enter the conversation. Ian explains that he will have help from his church in juggling his new job and the responsibility for the children. This alarms his parents.

> "Ian, have you fallen into the hands of some *sect?*" his father asked.
>
> "No, I haven't," Ian said. "I have merely discovered a church that makes sense to me, the same as Dober Street Presbyterian makes sense to you and Mom."
>
> "Dober Street didn't ask us to abandon our educations," his mother told him. "Of course we have nothing against religion; we raised all of you children to be Christians. But *our* church never asked us to abandon our entire way of life."
>
> "Well, maybe it should have," Ian said.
>
> His parents looked at each other.

His mother said, "I don't believe this. I do not believe it. No matter how long I've been a mother, it seems my children can still come up with something new and unexpected to do to me."[2]

Tyler's narrative deftly evokes two kinds of churches, two kinds of Christianity. One kind, Dober Street Presbyterian, supports people's customary and established ways of life and provides a chapel for their religious needs and rituals. The other one, the Church of the Second Chance, challenges that same way of life and proposes an alternative. It is lived in community together. The exchange between Ian and his parents resonates with the call of Jesus to various people in the New Testament, beginning with his first disciples. "Come, follow me," said Jesus to Peter and Andrew, James and John, who then did "abandon" their entire way of life to follow Jesus.

There are virtues and dangers in both kinds of churches. While the Church of the Second Chance turns out to be benign if quirky, we are all aware from both literature and life of the ways that the more demanding congregation, what Ian's father terms "a sect," can go astray and become destructive. But Tyler's story also suggests the anemia that exists in at least some, perhaps many, long-established churches in the mainline Protestant tradition. Such churches often seem to lack the capacity to change and to transform lives. They ask little of their adherents, and it can seem as though there is not much at stake in such churches or in the faith they foster. That faith is what I have termed "civic faith." For civic faith, religion — specifically Christianity — easily becomes an adjunct to a person's existing way of life and not a new or a different way of life.

That many mainline Protestant congregations became institutions of conventional, low-demand "civic faith" testifies to the perils of Christendom, of the meshing of religion, culture, class, and citizenship that I described in the first conversation. But beyond this sociological dimension, another question and a deeper, more theological dimension emerges: "Where can I find the living God?" Martin Luther, the scrupulous monk whose own crisis of faith precipitated the Protestant Reformation, is said to have asked, "Where can I find a loving God?" Luther had come to despair in his efforts to win God's love through his rectitude and works of faith. Luther's question remains a compelling ques-

2. Anne Tyler, *Saint Maybe* (New York: Ballantine Books, 1991), p. 127.

tion today, and the conviction of God's love for us and for the world God has created is both axiomatic and powerful.

Yet I have come to think that the question for our own time is a different one. Not so much "Where can I find a loving God?" but "Where can I find a living God, or *the* living God?" Where can I meet and be met by a God whose presence, power, mystery, and mercy are real, palpable, and life-changing? Is there a church where they don't simply talk *about* God as a kind of interesting concept that provides a stained-glass backdrop for middle-class morality, but where people *experience* God and where faith is a relationship to be confessed and celebrated?

As the contemporary culture wars have shaped the church and religion, it seems that the two usual sides have taken two predictable positions, mirror images of each other. One portrays and understands God as all-loving all the time, accepting us no matter what. But this God is not capable of actually doing much, if anything. "Here we believe in a loving God, not a judging one" is the way it is often put. God is like an indulgent grandparent, loving but ineffective. The other side portrays and understands God as powerful but picky: God only loves certain people, those who have the right faith, lifestyle, faith experience, or faith words. Most everyone else can (and will) go to hell.

I stand in the mainline tradition that believes in both a God whose embrace is wide, wider than our own, and in a biblical tradition that understands that ultimate "judgment is the Lord's." It is not up to us to decide who is in and who is out. But because I am seeking the renewal of that tradition and have a lover's quarrel with it, I recognize the truth of Anne Tyler's critique. We speak too readily of a loving God who forgives all and everything and expects nothing. At times we seem to have lost the words and way to speak of a living God who just might ask us to abandon our entire way of life.

Will Willimon tells the story of a youth pastor who was planning a Bible study on Mark's story of the baptism of Jesus. Typical of Mark's terse and powerful style, he reports that, when Jesus came up out of the water, "He saw the heavens *torn apart*" (the Greek word is *schizomei*, literally "torn apart"). The youth group members were responding to the Bible study the way youth group members often do, with indifference bordering on sullenness. So the pastor, eager to provoke some sort of response, said: "This is amazing, truly! Look at this: Mark says the heavens have been torn apart. Do you know what that means? That

means that now we all have direct access to God. There's nothing between us and God! Isn't that wonderful?"

"No, that's not what it means," said a young man, shifting in his
seat.

The pastor was nonplussed.

"What," he said to the young man, "you know Greek?"

"Yeah," said the kid. "*Schizomei,* torn apart. It means that now God
can get at us. It means that *now no one is safe.*"

It sometimes seems that the achievement of all socially established
religions is to render God "safe." Thus pastors labor to tell people that
God is all loving all the time, and we can go directly to God, and "isn't
that wonderful?" Perhaps we would do better, at least some of the time,
to speak of the God who is not safe or comfortable or predictable, but of
the God whose love is a refining fire and whose grace turns our world
upside down. As I say to students in my preaching classes, "The parables of Jesus are like hand grenades. They blow up our known worlds
and fixed ideas. But too often we preachers make the mistake of throw-
ing our own bodies on the grenade to protect our congregations from
the explosion. We turn deeply provocative parables into predictable
moral lessons."

Flannery O'Connor, a novelist writing a generation before Anne
Tyler, offered the following critique of mainline religion in the 1950s:

> One of the effects of modern liberal Protestantism has been gradu-
> ally to turn religion into . . . therapy, to make truth vaguer and vaguer
> and more and more relative, to banish intellectual distinctions, to de-
> pend on feeling instead of thought, and gradually to come to believe
> that God has no power, that he cannot communicate with us, cannot
> reveal himself to us, indeed has not done so and that religion is our
> own sweet invention.[3]

O'Connor sees the way that religion becomes less and less about a provocative and demanding God, about who God is and what God requires
of us, and more and more about us, what we want, and what or who we
want God to be. But when God is reduced to our own wants, desires, or

3. Flannery O'Connor, quoted in Fleming Rutledge, "A New Liberalism of the
Word," in *Loving God with Our Minds,* ed. Michael Welker and Cynthia A. Jarvis (Grand
Rapids: Eerdmans, 2004), p. 252.

self-image writ large, God is no longer a living God, and God is no lon-ger the God disclosed to us in Scripture.

Of course, this is not a new problem. It is as old as humankind, as ancient as Scripture itself. Human beings are forever fashioning gods that will serve them, rather than themselves serving the living God. That this is a long-standing distortion of faith, however, does not make it any less contemporary. Where the contemporary tendency to stress a vague, loving God at the expense of the living God comes to the fore is in worship and preaching. By definition, the focus of worship is God: worship is to be in the presence of God, to listen for God's Word to us, and to hear a message of, about, and from God. To worship is to enter into a zone of risk, a place and time where we might be changed. When religion becomes conventional, as in Tyler's depiction of Dober Street Presbyterian, or therapeutic, as in O'Connor's indictment, it becomes less a message about God and more a message about us. It may extol "the kind of church we are," or "the wonderful people who belong here," or the causes and enthusiasms we share at the moment. Or it may speak in the imperative voice and focus on what we are to think or feel, and provide a kind of weekly spiritual "to-do list." But worship as being with God and hearing the God message is lost. This may render worship safe and predictable, but it also renders it boring. It does not provoke, evoke, liberate, or save. "Changing the conversation" means, in part, declaring and knowing that we serve not only a friendly, loving God, but also a living God who can "get at us."

Our conviction that we serve a living God and our experience of worship and preaching as proclamation of the message — the truth — about God cuts across the usual liberal-conservative, right-left, red-blue polarities. At least it can, and it should! In the end, the living God is neither our version of liberal or conservative, neither a Democrat nor a Republican. By definition, God transcends the given categories of our experience and is capable of opening our eyes to see a new world not constrained by our prejudices and agendas. If mainline congregations that emphasize generous engagement in the world and justice and ser-vice to others are to thrive, they will do so because they experience God as *both* living and loving, and because they offer worship that is an en-counter with the living God.

In his book *Excellent Protestant Congregations*, television producer Paul Wilkes comes to a telling conclusion. Referring to mainline decline,

Wilkes says: "But to bemoan the mixture of institutional chaos and indi-vidual confusion that has accompanied the collapse is to miss the point: People are focusing less on church, and more on God." Wilkes continues with observations that resonate with Anne Tyler's fictional description. "People realize that window dressing is not enough — for no one is look-ing in the window anymore. People want to see and experience what's in the store, not simply be its lifeless mannequins. In place of that static window dressing on display each week is the possibility of a loving pres-ence not only for that Sunday hour, but throughout the week."[4]

Elemental to congregational vitality, to a new heart, and to chang-ing the conversation is getting the focus of our preaching, worship, and life together on God: who God is, what God has done, what God is do-ing, and what God has promised. God and the message about God is the first — and the last — word. It is only the second word that is about us. Such is the grammar of the gospel: first comes the word of God's amaz-ing (and troubling) grace; second comes the word about our response. Or as one reliable aphorism puts it, "Salvation is all about grace; ethics is all about gratitude."

For Reflection and Discussion
- When was the last time you experienced worship as provocative? Why?
- If Dober Street Presbyterian and the Church of the Second Chance are thought of as two ends of a spectrum, where on the spectrum would you place your church?

Scripture: Its Power and Purpose

The setting was the congregation's summer family camp. I had talked the planning team, not without some difficulty, into including a morn-ing Bible study for adults, adults who were used to doing their own thing while their children went to the children's program. We were working with the lectionary texts for the coming fall. The text that par-ticular morning was 1 Thessalonians 1:1-10. After Paul's words of ad-dress and greeting, verses 4-5 read: "For we know, brothers and sisters

---

4. Paul Wilkes, *Excellent Protestant Congregations* (Louisville: Westminster/John Knox, 2001), p. 158.

beloved by God, that he has chosen you, because our message of the gospel came to you not in word only, but also in power and in the Holy Spirit and with full conviction; just as you know what kind of persons we proved to be among you for your sake." After a few words of background, I invited people to share the words or phrases that spoke to them, words that touched or disturbed them. "'Chosen,'" said one woman, "what does that mean? I'm not sure I like the sound of it." Another person said, "I like the 'beloved by God' part."

Then a man, a middle-aged college professor, spoke: "It almost sounds like what Paul calls 'the gospel' is not so much words or ideas but a power or a force that does things."

"I think that's right," I replied. "I'm curious, what strikes you about that?"

"Well," said the scholar and teacher, "I guess I got into teaching because I believed that ideas had that power, that they could change lives, but now I'm not so sure. Everything seems to be about requirements, getting on to the next thing. It's as if we keep ourselves busy so that our lives won't be changed."

It seems to me that this insightful person had heard Paul correctly, that the gospel is not simply words or abstract ideas, but a power, a power that does create and change things. And he had also perceptively diagnosed the ways we find for protecting ourselves from encounter.

In an important essay, entitled "A New Liberalism of the Word," Fleming Rutledge observes:

> Underlying all of this is the question of power, of *dunamis*. The idea that the Word of God is powerful *in and of itself* has been fading in the mainlines for a long time. I am reminded of a characteristic locution in the African-American churches. A church member will say, "Who is going to bring the message today?" or "Thank you, Reverend, for bringing the message." We don't say that in the mainlines. We say, "Who's preaching today?" or "Thank you for the sermon." The idea of a message coming *with its own power* seems to lie outside our set of convictions; yet the entire biblical story is founded on that reality, and without it, the essential meaning of biblical revelation is lost.[5]

5. Rutledge, "A New Liberalism of the Word," p. 253.

There is an inextricable connection between the preceding section of this conversation, a living God, and this question of the power and the purpose of Scripture. Is Scripture, and its interpretation in study and proclamation in preaching, a word from the living God to God's people, or are they some interesting ideas that you might consider or that could make your life a little better (or not)? That is, is the focus on us ("what does this do for me?" or "did I like the preacher and her sermon?") or on God and what God is saying to us?

As with other things, Scripture itself has, of course, become a football in the culture wars, with each side offering its own skewed understanding of the disputed texts. On the right, Scripture is heralded as the "literal and inerrant" truth that is to be heard and obeyed without question or interpretation: "God said it; I believe it; that settles it." This formulation wholly neglects the origins of Scripture, and it dismisses the fact that interpretation is not only inevitable but required. "I don't interpret the Bible," intoned one conservative minister, "I just tell people what it says!" Such clergymen wield the Bible as a weapon in larger fights over authority and social control.

On the other side, and perhaps in reaction to turning the Bible into a war club that sanctions human authority and ideology, the liberal mainline tends to spend a great deal of time applying a hermeneutic of suspicion to Scripture, looking for whose interests are being served and how texts can be deconstructed along such lines. While this kind of study is not without value, it tends to leave the church with little to go on, as one can see from the very few words that one such interpreting group, the Jesus Seminar, attributes to Jesus in the Gospels. This deconstructionist approach comes to view the Bible as the product of power politics in the early church rather than as a product of the Holy Spirit's interaction with the lives and struggles of the early people of faith, or as God's word for people of faith today. The upshot is a reflexive distrust of Scripture alongside a similarly reflexive but certainly odd trust in whatever this approach presents as the latest "secret" or "lost" text, whether that be the Gospel of Thomas, the Gospel of Judas, or even something fictional like Dan Brown's *The Da Vinci Code*.

The results of this polarized situation are predictable: rather than reading, studying, or meditating on Scripture, and rather than struggling with the text for preaching, many have come to reify the Bible as an icon or symbol in the culture wars. What is the Bible, and what does it mean to call it "Scripture"? Clergy and teaching elders need to engage such questions on a steady basis as part of the teaching office of the church. Even more importantly, the people of congregations need to be engaged with Scripture through experiences such as the spiritual practice of *Lectio Divina,* group study, "through the Bible in one year" classes, and biblically grounded and inspired preaching. Neither the Christian faith nor the church can be sustained without regular and powerful interaction with the church's authorizing story and the God who speaks and acts through it. Ironically, however, a movement that began with the rediscovery of Scripture and a call to make it available to all people — that is, the Protestant Reformation — has devolved in the modern era to the point where only (seminary-trained) professionals are deemed competent to read or interpret the Bible. North Americans can learn from the model of Latin America's "Christian Base Communities," where ordinary Christians read, study, and apply Scripture to life. (The revolutionary implications of this practice were recognized by authorities in some of those countries, and they put an end to it!)

The questions of the power and purpose of the Bible is a conversation ripe for the church to change, rather than allowing the culture, and its wars, to script this conversation for us. While I do not have the space in this book to give a full and adequate response to the question about what the Bible is, and what it means to refer to it as "Scripture," I can point to a useful, if limited, analogy that might help us understand the purpose of Scripture: the Declaration of Independence, the Constitution, and the Bill of Rights — the founding documents of the United States. These are not the only such documents in the world. Americans can learn from similar documents that have been drawn up by other nations, just as Christians can learn from the sacred texts of other faiths. But these are the documents that remind us of *our* particular identity and the *constituting* norms and story of our identity. In a similar way, one can speak of the Bible as "the church's book," a book and story that remind us who we are and whose we are. The church that forgets Scripture forgets who it is and who God is, for Scripture conveys the story of our God and the patterns of God's activity. At the same time, our Scriptures are also the product of a thousand years of human life and history, and they require study and interpretation. Their meaning is not by and large self-evident. Therefore, as the great preacher Harry Emerson Fosdick said three generations ago, and as New Testament scholar Marcus

Borg has repeated more recently, we must take Scripture "seriously but not literally."[6]

While the Protestant Reformer John Calvin understood the term "the Word of God" to have several meanings, he argued that the Word of God is not only or primarily the printed words on the pages of the Bible. Rather, Calvin maintained that the Word of God is an occurrence, or event, that happens when the same Spirit that was present to the one who wrote is present to those who hear or read. In other words, the Word of God is a dynamic interaction of the Holy Spirit and the words of the biblical text in the vessel of the believing community. Moreover, that community, the church, depends for its very life on this living and lively Word, and this Word, as that college professor at the summer camp Bible study noted, has power! This is a power that is capable of calling worlds into being (Gen. 1), of giving life to the dead (Ezek. 37; Rom. 4), and enacting a new creation (2 Cor. 5; Rev. 21). The Gospel of John tells us that this Word is Jesus Christ: "And the Word became flesh and lived among us, and we have seen his glory" (John 1:14). And this Word that is Jesus Christ is mediated to us through the words of Scripture. If the churches are to gain a new heart and a new mind, Scripture remains a powerful and indispensable instrument of open-heart surgery.

For Reflection and Discussion

- How would you describe your own present relationship with the Bible?
- What have you experienced that has helped that relationship grow and deepen?

Evangelism Begins at Home

Sometime during the 1980s most mainline Protestant denominations "rediscovered" evangelism. Fifteen or twenty years into a downward spiral in membership numbers, some in the mainline church proposed evangelism as the way to turn things around. It didn't work. One way to describe why this sudden rediscovery of evangelism did not work is to use Heifetz's "technical problem/adaptive challenge" distinction. "Evan-

---

6. Borg, *Meeting Jesus (Again) for the First Time.*

gelism" was put forward as the known solution (it was also a series of techniques) to the clear problem of membership decline. It was to be carried out by experts and authorities, that is, clergy, denominational professionals, and specially trained volunteers or staff. But the mainline churches' situation was more complex and challenging — and frankly, more interesting — than that. Membership losses were more than a technical problem: they signaled an adaptive challenge brought on by the end of American Christendom and the waning of modernity.

Another way to explain why evangelism didn't work in the 1980s is that what we really meant by "evangelism" too often was "getting new members." This is not only a distortion of evangelism but a self-serving one at that. Not everyone, of course, was approaching evangelism that way; many were doing fine, gospel-centered work. But it was to little avail because the prevailing understanding of evangelism equated it with "getting new members."

At about that time (the early 1980s) I began a ministry in a new congregation, my second parish, which was a church with a proud history of social activism. I suggested that we incorporate into our regular worship service the "Greeting of Peace," a liturgical practice of the early church in which sisters and brothers in the community of faith greet one another with the gift of peace that Christ gives. Following a prayer of confession and the declaration of forgiveness, people were invited to greet one another, saying, "The peace of God be with you," or "The peace of Christ be with you," to which the response was, "and also with you." Simple enough. Not long after we began this practice, a woman who had been a ten-year member of that congregation said to me, "This is amazing! I don't think I've ever heard us use the word 'God' out loud with one another in this church before!" This may sound improbable to some readers, but it is a true story.

I tell this story to make the point that is the thesis of this section: I have come to the conclusion that we have gotten the focus for evangelism wrong. Evangelism is not, first of all, about others or outsiders or the "unchurched." The first people to be evangelized — that is, touched and transformed by the good news of God — are us, the existing congregations, the church, the *insiders*. In many long-established mainline and civic-faith congregations, attempting to do evangelism by asking people to go out to the "unchurched" and sharing the gospel has been a bit like asking nonreaders to tell other nonreaders about the great joy of books. Or like asking people who, though they have heard Shakespeare mentioned positively all their lives, have never themselves seen or read a play by Shakespeare to go out and tell others about the beauty and power of Shakespearean drama.

Perhaps this sounds unkind or judgmental. But I am not saying that, because we have in some cases never spoken about God to one another, or have not heard and received the good news of the gospel, we are therefore "bad" people. No, in most cases we are "good" people, that is, in the sense of being decent, caring, helpful, and moral. Some churches were full of extraordinarily fine and good people, and this was certainly true of my congregation referred to above. But none of these things means that we actually have a conscious and formed relationship with God, that we have some experience of the living Christ of which we are aware and about which we are articulate, or that we have any real notion of what is meant by "the Good News of the gospel." I have heard someone put it this way: "Just as sitting in the garage does not make you a car, sitting in church does not make you a Christian."

Civic faith did not require or entail a relationship with God or a lived experience of the gospel. In fact, keeping faith *civil* and socially acceptable may seem to disallow such experiences or at least require that you keep them strictly to yourself. For these reasons, according to missiologist Darrell Guder, it is the church and congregations that need conversion. Guder tells a poignant story that caught him "up short." A seminary student, doing field work, came back with this observation: "I see a lot of people in the church who don't have any experience of the blessing of the gospel anymore but are still trying to do mission."[7] When this is the case, mission, service, and outreach are like a cut flower: they are neither rooted and nurtured in God's grace and presence nor in our own experience and understanding of the gospel.

The mainline churches abandoned the evangelistic efforts of the 1980s because we had the wrong target audience — the "unchurched." The correct target audience for evangelism, in many instances, should have been the "churched," the congregations and members (and clergy) of our established churches. When our own faith is deepened as

---

7. Guder, *The Continuing Conversion of the Church* (Grand Rapids: Eerdmans, 2000), pp. 149-51.

we gain new hearts, as we learn the gospel story, and as we are ourselves converted to the gospel of God's grace in Jesus Christ, we will
not only have something to share with others, but reason to do so. A
related miscue of our earlier efforts at evangelism was that we tended
to think of evangelism as a particular program of the church, complete
with a budget line item and numerical goals. We formed committees
or assigned "evangelism" to an existing committee; or we hired staff
people who had evangelism as part of their portfolio. By and large, this
did not work either. The whole life of the church needs to be "evangelical" in the best sense of that word, that is, infused with the Good News,
the message of God.

In particular, worship is always an *evangelical* moment and engagement. This does not mean that we have to single out or target visitors or
the "unsaved" with an "altar call." But it means that our worship is evangelical in the sense that it claims that Christ, not Caesar, is Lord. True
evangelicalism claims that God is God, and not one of the great or small
powers we mistake for God is God: nation, family, money, success, the
American way of life, and so on. Worship in this truly evangelical sense
is always "spiritual warfare," where we engage the demonic powers that
diminish, distort, and disfigure life — and our own particular lives —
and we focus our lives on what is worthy of our worship, what is true,
and what is truly God.

Evangelism is not something we assign to a particular program,
staff person, or line item in the budget. It is hearing, receiving, and telling the good news about what God has done, is doing, and will do. This
is what the church is about. It is part of all that we do, and evangelism
is, in particular, central to the church's worship.

There may be a danger implicit in my contention that "evangelism
begins at home": saying that might lead to a focus only on ourselves and
our own faith. This is not my intention, and it would be a mistake, because a choice or polarity between "for us" and "for others" is a false
choice. A living, life-changing faith will always be expressed in concern
and love for others. My point is a simple one: we must not reduce evangelism to "getting more members" or "new member outreach." Evangelism in its true sense of hearing and receiving the Good News of the
gospel, with its resulting deepening of our relationship with God and
with the community of faith, needs to begin with our own congregations, or we will have nothing to share with others.

For Reflection and Discussion

- What pops into your mind when you hear the word "evangelism"?
- Think of, or tell of, an experience when someone shared something of his or her faith and experience of God with you in ways that were real and meaningful.

Theology: From Professional to Amateur

I recently visited one of Seattle's so-called emerging churches. Meeting in a warehouse-type building in an industrial area of the city, it hardly looked like "church" as I knew it. After fifteen minutes or so of praise music, as well as traditional hymns accompanied by a rock band, the preacher appeared and began an hour-long sermon on a topic that was part of a series he called "Who Did Christ Die For?" He drew on Augustine and Calvin and several more contemporary theologians, such as John Stott. I don't know whether I agreed with the preacher's conclusions, but the sermon was seriously theological. Looking around at members of the congregation, I marveled at the number of twenty- and thirty-somethings in attendance, many of them taking notes. If I had preached a sermon so explicitly theological in nature and of that length, would the congregation I served have been interested?

In a recent essay, the Pulitzer-Prize-winning novelist Marilynne Robinson comments on the "rise in this country of a culture of Christianity that does not encourage thought." She says: "I do not intend this as a criticism of the so-called fundamentalists only, but more particularly of the mainline churches, which have assiduously culled out all traces of the depth and learnedness that were for so long among their greatest contributions to American life."[8]

During the period of modernity we somehow lost the notion that theology is an appropriate concern of the church and wisdom proper to the life of every believer. In good part, this reflects the penchant of modernity for professionalizing various aspects of life and placing them in the purview of experts. Theology was something done by professional theologians, experts, and authorities, and they were located in seminaries or universities. Such professional theologians might, on occasion,

---

8. Marilynne Robinson, "Hallowed Be Thy Name," *Harper's* (July 2006): 20.

venture out into the church to give a lecture. Once or twice in their careers they might write a book intended for a popular or lay audience. By and large, though, professional theologians were playing a different game: it was a game in which the players were other professional theologians, the language was incomprehensible to ordinary people, and the score was kept on résumés and lists of publications. Furthermore, clergy, even though they had taken theology classes in seminaries and studied with theologians, did not think of themselves as "theologians." Once they had completed the required theology courses in their seminary training, many clergy did not find much use for theology. It seemed too technical, abstract, and preoccupied with methodology, and thus not especially helpful in the daily life and work of the pastor.

My proposal for this fourth aspect of getting "a new heart" is to declare that the day of "theology for professionals only" is over — and it's high time! It is time for a shift in how we think of and practice theology, a shift from professional to amateur. This may alarm some of my readers for whom the word "amateur" suggests something like "half-baked," a theology that is poorly or irresponsibly done by theological autodidacts. That is a danger, of course, but that is not what I mean by "amateur." Properly understood, doing something as an amateur means doing something for the love of that thing or activity itself. Theology done for the love of it!

Underlying this proposal of a shift from professional to amateur as the primary locus of theological practice is a different understanding and definition of theology. I am using "theology" here not in the sense of an academic discipline; rather, I want to define theology as, in the words of theologian Edward Farley, "wisdom proper to the life of every believer." In such an understanding, theology is not primarily a guild requiring professional credentials and holding annual society meetings. Theology is a way of seeing life, a way of seeing ourselves, our neighbors, and our world. It is the lens through which we view life and according to which we live life.[9]

Our core theological convictions speak of the nature of Christianity

---

9. See Anthony B. Robinson, *What's Theology Got to Do with It? Convictions, Vitality, and the Church* (Herndon, VA: Alban Institute, 2006). In that book I seek to articulate the core convictions of the Christian faith and to demonstrate how they shape or "regulate" the life of healthy and vital congregations.

as a revealed religion (revelation), Scripture and its role in the church, God the Creator, the Trinity, human sin, the person and work of Jesus Christ, the Holy Spirit, the church and Christian life, and hope. I have understood and practiced ordained ministry as that of a field- or congregation-based teacher and scholar, an understanding of ministry that might be described as "rabbinic." I have found that bringing core Christian conviction into dialogue with the lives of believers, the life of a congregation, and the issues and experiences of the society as a whole is not only possible but is imperative. This is at the core of why I propose that theology belongs to the life of the church and can be "wisdom proper to the life of every believer."

The young people who sat in that emerging church in Seattle were looking, I imagine, for truth and meaning to guide and inform their lives. They were looking for a place to stand. There are many competitors for their hearts and minds in the postmodern world in which they live. Moreover, there are corrosive forces that daily undermine personal integrity and covenanted relationships such as marriage, and that can reduce life to acquiring and having "stuff." While some churches teach in ways that are ideological and even bigoted, that need not be the case in the church that is truly grounded evangelically and theologically. Theology as wisdom proper to the life of the believer can be taught and lived in congregations in ways that invite people to lives that are coherent, purposeful, and joyful. Theology — what we believe about God, ourselves, and human life — is the birthright of all the baptized and can be done by everyone for the love of it.

For Reflection and Discussion

- Do a word association with "theology." What comes to mind for you?
- If your pastor were to say, "This [the forming and sustaining of Christians] is going to take more than one hour a week," would you agree, disagree, be open to exploring that, or would you leave to find another church?

A Concluding Word

Often efforts at congregational renewal are boiled down to initiating a new program or following a new formula. Not only do such efforts seldom deliver what they promise, they protect us from deeper transformation, from gaining a new heart and a new mind. In this chapter I have sought to provoke a conversation about such a transformation and about the four chambers, so to speak, of a new heart: an encounter with the living God and the message of and about God; the power and purpose of Scripture; evangelism for the "churched"; and reclaiming theology as "wisdom proper to the life of believers." These are four aspects of one whole *transformation,* that is, being "formed anew" or "formed over" by the living God.

Some readers may say, "Great, but tell us how." I will turn to adult Christian formation as an adaptive challenge in a later chapter, and there I will suggest specific steps and strategies. But this transformation, getting a new heart, is at the center of mainline Protestant congregations, and it is not reducible to a formula or recipe. Different congregations and their leaders will find various ways to go about this. Moreover, it is more a matter of an orientation than a program or plan. Finally, and most important, transformation is not something *we* do, certainly not something we do by ourselves. It is God's work. It is God who works transformation. Getting a new heart means opening ourselves to God, seeking God, turning to God, surrendering to God, and relying on God. It does not mean giving up responsibility, but it does mean surrendering our illusion of control. It means letting God be God for us.

Who Shall Lead Them?

"We have a leadership problem here!"

"What we need is a leader!"

"If this church is going to make progress, we need effective leadership, and right now we don't have it."

"Give us leadership!"

These are common cries in the church, and not only in the church. Wherever one turns these days — government and politics, education, business, healthcare, the military, universities — one hears the call for and the concern about leadership. Is leadership the problem? Is effective leadership the solution? Yes and no.

Yes, because leaders are critically important. If any group or institution is to make progress on its more important challenges, capable leaders are required. But no, because "leadership" is not a silver bullet, not a magic solution. We can't simply replace one pastor, principal, or president with another and expect that suddenly everything will be back to smooth sailing. We do need effective leaders who will guide the ship amid the sea change of our new time. But leaders, by definition, do not do it alone. If we imagine that putting the right leader in place will magically solve all our problems, erase all our challenges, and return us to a former golden age, we need to think again. If we recognize that effective leaders are crucial in helping congregations deal with their most pressing problems and engage their most critical challenges, then we are correct. Leaders are important, in fact, so important that leadership is the next critical conversation.

At the church's first Pentecost (Acts 2), two key questions frame the narrative. The first question, "What does this mean?" was the subject of our first conversation. Both Conversations 2 and 3 engaged the second question at Pentecost, "What, then, shall we do?" "Who shall lead them?" becomes the crucial question as the story of Acts unfolds, and it is also crucial today if we are to make progress on the urgent challenges of our time.

Leadership: Three Components

When I speak of "leadership," I am not speaking of pastoral leadership alone. Pastoral leadership is one component — indeed, a critical one — of the three key parts of congregational leadership, but it is only one part of the package. In addition to faithful and effective pastoral leadership, two other important components emerge: the leadership team and the congregation's governance structure. We need to emphasize and gradually develop all three parts of the leadership package in order to engage the challenges of this new time.

If a pastor tries to do it alone, or is *expected* to do it alone, without developing a leadership team, leadership will not only wear that pastor down and eventually out, but new life and renewal will not have been broadly enough embraced throughout the congregation to be sustainable. A leadership team is necessary in order for the congregation to effect change in its direction and focus. In addition, pastoral leadership and the leadership team must be complemented by the congregation's governance and the formal leadership structure. Many congregations today are organized for and governed by structures that worked well in the previous era, the era of American Christendom and of modernity. They are not working so well today.

In this chapter, as I discuss each of the three parts of the leadership package, I will describe what effective leadership looks like and will suggest how to get there. One caveat: different denominations have different structures and offices, as well as different understandings of the pastoral role and office. For example, in my own denomination, the United Church of Christ, ordained ministers are members of the congregation but not typically voting members of the governing board, usually called a "church council." Ordained United Church of Christ clergy are usually ex officio members of the council. But among Presby-terians, for example, it is pretty much the opposite: ordained ministers do not hold membership in the congregation, but rather in the regional body, the presbytery. Not only are they voting members of the govern-ing board, the "Session" in Presbyterian churches, ordained clergy are the "ruling elders," that is, the chairpersons of the Session. The varia-tions continue as we include more denominations in the picture. Not only are there different denominational traditions, but individual con-gregations have different needs, contexts, and histories. I understand and acknowledge this variety, and I will depend on readers to adapt what follows to their particular contexts. While such variations in structure and tradition are real, the basics of leadership and the three parts of the leadership package remain pertinent and applicable.

For Reflection and Discussion
- In your view, what do leaders do?
- If denominations are, at least in part, leadership-providing systems, how effective is yours in this regard?

Pastoral Leadership

The reader will recall my discussion of Christendom in the first conver-sation. There I described an established church that was settled in what was considered a Christian culture. The purpose of the church and the role of its pastor were, first and foremost, to provide for and serve the religious needs of the congregation's members. Moreover, membership was much more of a social given. The questions were not so much "Are you a believer?" or "Are you a Christian?" as they were "Are you a Cath-olic or a Protestant?" and "Which church or denomination do you be-long to?"

While Christendom certainly produced some great social pioneers and church leaders, the role of parish clergy was not primarily that of a leader. Their role was to be a chaplain, one who provided for the reli-gious and spiritual needs of the members of the congregation, as well as of the wider community. Exaggerating to make a point, I might say that pastors in the Christendom era were similar to civil servants: they were not paid by the government (at least not in North America), but they were part of a given, habitual social structure that included church-going and membership and family affiliation along denominational lines. While some chaplains and de facto civil servants certainly had leadership gifts and capacities, these roles usually did not call forth or even reward leadership. Where the Christendom era did invite pastors to be leaders, it was usually as part of the established authority structure of a town or city. A pastor — or members of the town's clergy — might join the mayor, school principal, leading businesspeople, and the like, as part of the community leadership. But this was less a role of congregational leadership than being, by virtue of clerical office, part of an established town leadership, civic elite, or authority structure.

My point is simple: the roles and skills that served us well in the Christendom era are not especially helpful today. In fact, they may be counterproductive. The pastor who functions only as a chaplain who ministers to the needs of individuals and families within his or her congregation may be excellent in that regard but deficient as a congregational leader. Moreover, clergy who have been nurtured within Christendom and its ways, and are thus disposed to be de facto religious civil servants, may be ill equipped for the challenges of our new time. We may find more guidance for our future in looking to our distant past, the early, pre-Constantinian church, than in looking to our more recent past in American Christendom. To put it another way, pastors who would be leaders have to unlearn some old habits, habits of establishment, and learn new habits and skills to be pastoral leaders in a post-Christendom and postmodern world.

None of the Christendom roles for the clergy — chaplain to congregation and community, religious civil servant, part of the civic authority structure — represent the kinds of pastoral leadership we see exhibited in the book of Acts by the apostles and deacons. Leaders of that emerging church were understood as "prophets-like-Jesus" who helped newly emerging congregations learn who they were and why they existed. They were preachers and teachers of the faith who enabled congregations to negotiate change and their relationship to the larger culture and to the empire. They called people to faith in the Lord Jesus and challenged the lordship of Caesar. They did not prop up the established order; they boldly challenged it. Nor do the Christendom roles represent the kind of leadership that is implicit in the Pauline Epistles or in the Catholic Epistles of Peter, James, and John. Pastoral leaders in the emerging church of the New Testament are concerned to build up the body of Christ and equip the saints for ministry. Peter, Paul, James, Priscilla, Lydia, and John were all concerned with building up congregations of believers who were a light to the world and a leaven to society's loaf. In summary, the system that has existed in recent centuries has not called forth pastors who were leaders; in many ways, quite the opposite. But our new time requires just that: pastors who are leaders.

What is leadership, and how is it done? I have addressed these questions more extensively elsewhere,[1] but it may be useful to explore three key points here: first, a working definition of "leadership"; second, some characteristics of leaders; and third, congregational expectations.

Leadership: A Working Definition

While there is probably no single or complete definition of leadership, it is still important and useful for pastoral leaders to have some working definition of leadership as well as their own "leadership style." My working definition of leadership has been influenced by the work of Ronald Heifetz.[2] Leadership is not, in my judgment, coming into a situation with the answers or "the vision" and getting people to line up behind you. Leadership is mobilizing a congregation (be it small or large) to *engage its own most pressing problems and deepest challenges.* Sometimes today, amid the cry for leaders, we tend to look for the charismatic personality who has a compelling vision and the ability to get everybody fired up. I don't necessarily think of that as leadership because, while it may stimulate growth and productivity for a while, it makes a congregation overly dependent on that individual. When he or she goes, a congregation is often lost and there is a meltdown.

Leadership, as I would define it, builds capacity and sustainability within a congregation as it mobilizes a congregation to engage and make progress on its deepest challenges. Paul calls this "building up the body." Moreover, such leaders in the church context are also preachers

1. See Anthony B. Robinson, *Leadership for Vital Congregations* (Cleveland: Pilgrim Press, 2006).

2. See Ronald Heifetz, *Leadership without Easy Answers* (Cambridge, MA: Belknap Press, 1994); see also Heifetz, *Leadership on the Line* (Cambridge, MA: Harvard Business School Press, 2002).

and teachers who build up and lead the church on a theological basis. Leadership, as it is shown in the book of Acts, involves building up the body by sound teaching. In the church, leadership is not simply an application of techniques from the secular or business world. Leadership is rooted in the truth about God. Therefore, this conversation about leadership presupposes and builds on the previous conversation, "A New Heart."

To say that pastoral leaders mobilize congregations to engage their own most pressing problems and deepest challenges is *not* to say that pastoral leaders only work on or take their cues from what people in a congregation say are their problems and their challenges. Indeed, part of the task of leadership is reading the setting and congregation and framing and describing the problems and challenges accurately. The way congregations describe or name their own challenges is frequently part of the problem. So leadership may name problems and challenges that congregations did not know they had, or they may reframe the ones congregations have identified.

In addition to a working definition of leadership, pastors should have some notion of their own "leadership style." While there is no one correct leadership style, I would emphasize a few key skills to develop: asking good questions, seeing relationships between parts and the whole, developing and empowering leaders, stepping forward and taking risks when it is helpful and strategic to do so, and consistently articulating purpose and core values.

Let's unpack these elements briefly. Asking good questions is a key leadership skill, because leaders do not just provide answers — they ask important questions. I also emphasize perceiving relationships: that is, seeing how the parts fit into the whole, how a congregation works (or doesn't work) as a system. As part of my own leadership, I want to identify, call forward, and empower others who have leadership gifts and capacities. On occasion I will step ahead of the group, declare myself, and take the risks that are inherent in pointing the way. However, I try to use that style selectively, for a couple reasons. For one thing, as one wise mentor said, "If you get too far out in front of the people, they'll think you're the enemy and shoot you." Second, if a leader is on point all the time, it tends to disable the leadership of others and encourage dependency. Finally, I consider it my leadership role to remind a congregation (or other group) of its theologically and biblically informed purpose and core values. In other words, leadership should keep before the congregation the issues of "who are we?" (core values) and "why are we here?" (purpose). Congregations, like other organizations, tend to lose or misplace their purpose and forget who they are. Leaders are there to remind them of it.

Not only is it useful to have a working definition of leadership and some idea of the characteristics of their own leadership style, but pastoral leaders do well to pay attention to a congregation's expectations and to the particular setting and context in which they seek to lead. To put it in a slightly different way, leaders help congregations pay attention to their own definitions and expectations of leadership. Members of congregations too often voice a desire for "leadership" but have widely diverging, even contradictory, notions of what a leader will be and will do. In other words, congregations are ambivalent about leadership. They want leadership, and yet they don't want leadership. Part of true leadership is reading the context and helping people in congregations clarify their own expectations and attitudes about leadership.

What are pastors who are accustomed to being chaplains but not leaders to do? Such persons have a couple of options: they can go to a setting that requires a chaplain, whether it be a hospital, prison, nursing home, or another of the growing number of institutions that have "workplace chaplains"; or they can join the equally growing ranks of those who practice one-on-one spiritual direction as their vocation. These are valid and important ministries, but not ones that place a high priority on leadership. Alternatively, such persons can work on developing their leadership gifts and skills. Options here include working with a leadership coach or mentor, enrolling in a doctor of ministry program with a leadership emphasis, or joining a clergy group or seminar that focuses on leadership skills and strategies. These resources are increasingly available.

What are congregations that do not have effective pastoral leaders to do? Start by analyzing your own expectations. What does leadership mean to you? What are the most important challenges on which you as a congregation seek to make progress, and what kind of leadership do you need to accomplish that? Once you have reasonable clarity on these questions — and if you have a pastor who is not providing effective leadership — you again have a couple of options. You can encourage that person to grow as a leader and develop leadership capacities (see above) and support her or him in doing so. Or you can say, "It appears that we have not found a good match between your gifts and our needs," and conclude that relationship and seek new pastoral leadership that is a better match.

When a congregation seeks new pastoral leadership, it is important to do careful work on the front end, that is, before calling a new pastor. Typical and long-established congregations tend to look for someone "who fits in with us" or whom people find personally likable and appealing. While fit is important, it is even more important for congregations to ask a somewhat harder question as honestly as they can: "What are we trying to accomplish in the next three or five or ten years, and what kind of leadership do we need to do that?" Congregations looking for the kind of pastor who was effective thirty or forty years ago may call someone who is quite ineffective in this new time.

New leadership is critical and effective pastoral leadership a necessity if congregations are to make progress on the challenges of our time. Effective pastoral leadership does not mean that the person called has received a 100-percent approval rating or that everyone "likes" him or her (in fact, effective leaders will often experience resistance). It does mean that the leader should have a sense of direction, a passion about the church and the faith, and a capacity to help a congregation make progress on its most pressing problems and deepest challenges.

For Reflection and Discussion
- Think of someone you regard as an effective leader. What qualities stand out about that person and his/her leadership?
- Describe the expectations your congregation has for its pastor.

A Leadership Team

I have made the point that what congregations need, particularly those of the historic mainline Protestant denominations, is not simply a charismatic pastor, an exciting new program, a galvanizing mission project, or an ambitious goal for growth in membership. The challenges we face are deep, and we need a response that is deeper than any of those "quick fixes." The culture of the congregation needs to change. The shift is from a culture suited to the era of American Christendom, in which mainline Protestant churches were the religious establishment, to a culture that can engage the secular, pluralistic, postmodern, post-Christendom world in which we live and seek to be the church for this new age. Michael Foss describes such a shift emphasis this way: "from a culture of membership to a culture of discipleship."[3] In my book *Transforming Congregational Culture*, I have attempted to show, in key areas of congregational life, how we did church in an earlier time, and to suggest new ways of doing church — shifts in "congregational culture" — that are responsive to the new time in which God has placed us. For example, I spoke there of the shifts "from Christian education to Christian formation," from "board culture to ministry culture," and from "democracy to discernment."[4]

The point of this section of the conversation on leadership is a simple one: if a congregation is to succeed in making change in its culture, in its ways of doing church and being church, it needs to have a *leadership team*. To put that point negatively, this is not something a pastoral leader, even a most gifted one, can pull off alone. That is, it is not acceptable for even a very gifted person to say, in effect, "Watch me work." She or he must find ways to say, "Work with me," or "How can we work together on this?" As the preceding section of this conversation has indicated, effective and capable pastoral leadership is crucial for a congregation to make progress on these important challenges. A pastor who is simply a chaplain, though he or she may provide excellent pastoral care, will not be adequate to the task. A pastoral leader will help a congregation engage the key questions that mark the early chapters of the book of Acts: "What does this mean?" and "What, then, shall we do?" Or, in alternative, contemporary phrasing, "What's going on?" and "How do we respond?" In order to make progress on these questions and challenges, the congregation needs to build leadership capacity: leading cultural change in congregations requires a leadership team.

In order to develop such a team, many pastors will turn, quite understandably, to their churches' elected leaders and governing boards,

---

3. Michael Foss, *Power Surge: Six Marks of Discipleship for a Changing Church* (Minneapolis: Augsburg Fortress, 2000), pp. 11ff.

4. See Robinson, *Transforming Congregational Culture* (Grand Rapids: Eerdmans, 2003).

whether that body is called a church council, a session, a consistory, or something else. That could be the right move; however, if you are at an early stage in leading cultural change, it could prove to be a mistake. This is why I have two distinct sections in this chapter, one on the leadership team and the other on the governing board. In most congregations, the existing governing body was created for the earlier era of Christendom. If a pastor turns directly and only to that body to develop a leadership team, she may well run into a brick wall, because that group has not been created or trained to lead change in the system. By and large, governing boards are acculturated to maintain the present system and its ways of doing and being church. Though individual members of that board may be capable and of good intention, the system and its cultural ethos are oriented toward maintaining the status quo, not toward new learning, changing patterns of behavior and action, or making adaptive responses to a new time.

In due course it will be necessary to develop a governing body or board that is part of the change process and leadership team. But it may prove both wise and necessary at an early stage in the work of change to build a leadership team that is less formal in nature and more fluid in membership. Building such an ad hoc leadership team is the focus of this section; in the next section we shall turn to the governing board as part of the leadership package.

Let's clarify what I mean by "leadership team." I do not necessarily mean elected leaders, chairs of boards or committees, or presidents of guilds or fellowships in the congregation. I have in mind something less formal: a fluid group of people who have some capacity to influence others in the congregation and who share, or have the potential to share, a common vision. Who would be on such a team? There are no hard and fast rules on this. In my experience, it includes members of the church staff, laity who are what one might describe as "opinion leaders," and a certain number of the newer members.

Let's look at each of those categories briefly in turn. Midsize (200-500 members) and larger (500+ members) congregations will typically have a church staff that may include some or all of the following: a business manager, staff members in music and the arts, associate or assistant ministers, lay ministers, and so on. Members of the church staff need to be part of the leadership team. This does not mean that they all have to think alike; but it does mean that they should share core values and have enough in the way of common experience to develop trust and understanding with each other. Pastoral leaders can develop this capacity among staff by playing a role in the calling and hiring process, by working on team-building in regular staff meetings, by sharing and discussing common readings or other relevant material, by taking periodic retreats, and by taking "field trips" to other congregations. Again, the point is not for a church staff to march in lockstep, but that such a group may develop, often over time, a shared sense of the church's purpose, vision, and values.

Another kind of person who should be part of this informal leadership team is the church member who is an opinion leader in the congregation. This is normally someone who has been around for a while, who has played several roles in the congregation, and who has come to be trusted and respected by others for his judgment and character. A pastoral leader will cultivate relationships with such informal congregational leaders through pastoral visits and one-on-one conversations, inviting such people to participate in study groups and asking them to play a leadership role as a congregation begins to explore "what's going on?" and "how do we respond?" People like this often respond well to being given a stimulating book with the invitation, "Let's talk about this after you've had a chance to read it and think about it."

A third category of people who might be a part of this fluid and informal leadership team would be newer members of the congregation who have interest and energy. Why newer members? Because they see things that those who have been around a long time may no longer see. Because they, "not knowing any better," often ask the right questions, such as "Why do we do this?" and "Is this the best way to do this?" and "Is this working?" A pastoral leader may do similar things with these alert and capable newer members to cultivate relationships and build capacities: one-on-one conversations, shared readings and conversations, a small group gathering for conversation and prayer. Sometimes pastoral leaders err by leaning too heavily on relatively newer members. There needs to be a balance of established and trusted opinion leaders and newer members with fresh perspectives. Too much of either one will undermine the work and the pastoral leadership.

Does this leadership team meet as a group? It may or it may not. It may meet as a kind of "kitchen cabinet" or a "think tank"; but if it does, it should probably keep a low profile and remain low-key. It may meet occasionally as a group that is personally invited by the pastor with stated intentions to "think out loud together" and to "give the pastor feedback and perspective." The point is to exercise informal leadership rather than formal leadership. What would this look like, this exercise of "informal leadership"? It may mean that persons who are part of this team speak up in adult classes, small groups, congregational meetings, or informal gatherings in ways that change the conversation and move it forward. It may mean that members of this informal team do step forward to play key leadership roles when those arise. It may mean that such persons take leadership roles in stewardship and giving. The point is that you need more than just the pastor saying, "We aren't in Kansas anymore, Toto," as well as getting excited about new directions and ways of being and doing church in our new time.

It may be possible, over time, to phase out such an informal leadership team as the formal structure of leadership becomes oriented to a new role and to new directions and to ongoing renewal for a congregation. But in the earlier stages of such work, existing governing bodies are typically better at saying no than they are at saying yes; so turning to governing bodies too early may be counterproductive. At the same time, to neglect or to make an end run around the existing and formal leadership is not wise and may even prove disastrous. It is a question of timing.

The Governing Board

The third part of the leadership picture is an effective governing board or formal leadership body. Many congregations, especially long-established ones, do not have an effective governing board. Such a group may exist on paper or in the organizational structure of the congregation, but the reality of it is nonexistent or ineffective. Why? There are several interrelated factors that contribute to this absence, but perhaps the most common is that what needs to be or is even intended to be a governing body has devolved into an information-sharing group that hears reports and stops at that.

Here's a fairly typical example. A certain congregation's governing body, on paper, is called the church council. It is made up of twenty-five members (which is too large; ten to fifteen is about right), and includes the officers of the church (5), the chairpersons of every standing board or committee (10), and then a cadre of "at-large" members (10). The council understands its role to be one of "communication and coordination." In practice, what this means is that the church council hears reports from the chairpersons of the various boards and committees. Occasionally someone will ask a question, but that is usually frowned on because there are so many reports to get through each month, and the meetings are already too long and deadly boring as it is. Every now and then the council, in an effort to actually do something, will foolishly plunge into the bailiwick of a particular committee member or staff member — with more or less disastrous results. In reality, there is little or no coordination. There may be a good deal of information shared, but it is unclear to what end. This brief description of the actual practice of many church councils, consistories, or sessions may seem to be a bit of an exaggeration, but not much!

Part of the reason that the governing body devolves into this role is that many congregations operate on the assumption that the best way to involve people in their faith and in the church is to get them to serve on a board or committee. Of course, this means that you end up with quite an array of boards and committees; and someone, it seems, needs to keep track of it all. But this assumption, that involvement equals church governance, needs to be questioned. In her book *Raising the Roof*, Alice Mann says: "Don't equate involvement with church governance. A good many congregations see an extensive committee structure as the best way to release member gifts for ministry. For the GI generation, this wasn't such a bad strategy. Subsequent generations of adults are less patient with institutional life. They want to participate in meaningful action."[5] In many congregations the board and committee structure can be streamlined significantly, and other forms of involvement can be developed.

But just because we want to re-examine the assumption that equates involvement with church governance does not mean that effective governance is not important. It may be — probably should be — streamlined, but effective governance and leadership is still needed. In fact, I would argue that it is needed now more than ever. The "get everybody on a committee" syndrome and its corollary, "governing board

5. Alice Mann, *Raising the Roof* (Herndon, VA: Alban Institute, 2001), p. 53.

Who Shall Them?   93

as information clearing-house," were designed to maintain a stable system during a different time, the era of American Christendom. But we do not live there any longer. Our new time presents congregations with significant and worthy challenges that require effective leadership and an effective governing body. It is time to move away from "governing board as information clearing-house" role to one that, along with pastoral leadership, gives effective leadership to the congregation. Another way to put this is that, at best, most such groups tended toward management, not leadership. Effective managers tend to think in the short term; they tend to think in terms of their part, not the whole; and they tend to think inside the box, not in terms of renewal. Effective leaders think longer term; they think systemically (that is, they see the relationship of the parts to the whole); and they think in terms of renewal. They are always asking, "How can we do better?"

The new role and responsibilities of the governing body are to govern and lead. Michael Foss sums it up this way: "A church board is responsible for the *governance* of the congregation and not the *operational administration* of the congregation. The board establishes policies, sets fiscal and personnel policies, approves the overall budget, and adopts the vision for the congregation."[6] In some respects, such a body more nearly resembles the effective board of a not-for-profit organization: it operates at a strategic and policy level, not at the level of operational administration. It has the responsibility for developing (ordinarily in consultation with both staff members and congregation) and implementing the vision through the staff and the structures of the church. In doing this work, it is guided by a clear sense of the overall purpose or mission of the congregation (a subject to which we will turn in the next chapter). For now the point is a simple one: the governing body exists to govern and to provide leadership.

A couple of things must happen in order for this change in the role and functioning of a church's governing body to be accomplished. The group must understand its role, which is to provide leadership, not merely to hear reports, govern, and set policy direction, that is, not merely to focus on operational administration. There are at least two other key steps: one involves the nominations or *selection process* for this governing group; the other involves the *training and formation* of

6. Foss, *Power Surge,* p. 140.

its members. Each of these processes requires some extended attention here, and I will discuss the selection process first.

Many congregations fill slots rather than call leaders. Along about November, members of the congregation will receive phone calls with a plea: "Listen, help me out here. I have two more slots to fill [on the _____ board or committee]. You can do it for two years, right?" This is called "filling slots" and is not an especially productive practice; it is better to call leaders.

Start by asking the pastor and associate pastor(s) who they believe are, or have the potential to be, the *spiritual leaders* of the congregation. Ask the same question of the congregation and of outgoing board members. Assemble a list of those persons who are thought of by those groups and individuals as actual or potential spiritual leaders of the congregation. Let the nominating committee itself add to the list the names of others whom they see as actual or potential spiritual leaders. Then it is time for discernment: the nominating committee seeks God's guidance in prayer and reflection about whom to call for this work. The next step is to approach people and invite them to consider this call to service. This is best done in person, not over the phone or by e-mail. The point is to move away from filling slots in order to complete the nominations committee's report, and rather to call leaders — spiritual leaders.

The subsequent step, one that is overlooked in most congregations, is the training and formation of these leaders. What do our called leaders need to know in order to be empowered for their ministry and effective in it? In my experience, training and formation, if they happen at all, are limited to such things as skills in leading meetings, parliamentary procedure, the church program and administrative calendar, and a look at the by-law description of the board, along with some "getting-to-know-you" activities. There is little or no formation that equips and empowers those who have been called to grow as spiritual leaders.

Pastors need to begin to see the spiritual formation of church leaders as a crucial part of their teaching ministry. Whether the setting is a three-day (Friday evening through Sunday) weekend retreat or a series of evening classes, no one should be seated on the governing body of a congregation without training and formation. What should the curriculum for such training and formation be? Such leaders need to be on board with the church's purpose (covered in the next chapter) and vision ("vision" = what God is calling us to do in the next three to five years).[7] But formation cannot stop there. It needs to include personal faith experience and sharing, plus a knowledge of the core theological convictions of the church, including its understanding of the person and work of Jesus Christ and the role and authority of Scripture. There needs to be some attention to church discipline, that is, how to handle conflict and complaints, as well as moral/ethical problems. Finally, the formation of leaders should include both denominational history/polity and attention to how our particular congregation is structured and does business. You may be thinking, "Well, that's a lot." Yes, but it should be seen as an opportunity rather than a burden. See it as part of the congregation's ministry of teaching and adult spiritual formation. If you want people to take a job and position seriously, then take the training and preparation for the work seriously.

Consider the alternative. In the absence of worthwhile and engaging training and formation for spiritual leadership, most people bring to the task the assumptions they have from other areas: business, civic and service groups, and not-for-profit organizations. There is much of value that can be drawn from such settings and experience, but there is nothing that is specifically Christian, biblical, spiritual, or theological. The result is that our leadership bodies in the congregation often are not informed by the Christian faith, and that seems to me a serious deficiency. In Acts 20:17-34, one of the most important texts in the New Testament regarding leadership, Paul speaks to the Ephesian elders of his leadership among them and of the leadership challenges they face. It is very clear in this reflection that Paul's own leadership is theologically informed, and that a central criterion for leadership in the church is "sound teaching," or, as Paul puts it, "declaring the whole message about God." In the church we must not separate leadership and theological content. Leaders are stewards of the mysteries of God, and thus they must be chosen from among the spiritually mature and must possess or have real interest in gaining a well-grounded and theologically informed faith.

In summary, we need an effective governing and leadership group in the congregation. We need an empowered and formed group of spiritual leaders who join the pastor or pastoral team in clarity about

---

7. Lovett Weems, *Taking the Next Step* (Nashville: Abingdon Press, 2003), p. 94.

church purpose and in advancing church vision. To get there, the governing board needs to be clear about its role and needs to move away from a passive role of listening to reports or attempting to manage operational administration. The nominations and recruitment process needs to be transformed from filling slots to calling leaders. And then the leaders need and deserve excellent training and spiritual formation opportunities.

As I have observed earlier in this chapter, when the governing board of the congregation is really functioning as a leadership team, the informal leadership team that I focused on in the middle section of this chapter may no longer be needed. That group may be an interim step, or it may continue as an informal advisory group, a kind of "kitchen cabinet" for the pastors and key elected and called lay leaders. But congregations that are going to be faithful and fruitful in this new time, and are going to face the challenges and make the most of the opportunities facing us in this new century, do require effective leadership. The church of this era needs both pastors who are leaders and also effective governing and leadership bodies of lay members.

For Reflection and Discussion
- Describe the process by which your congregation currently selects or nominates its leaders.
- In your opinion, what are the qualities of a spiritual leader?
- What do spiritual leaders need to know to be prepared and effective? In other words, what would be the components of a spiritual formation course or experience if you were to design it?

The Leadership Vacuum

At present, many congregations suffer from a leadership vacuum. Instead of pastoral leaders, they have chaplains; instead of governing boards, they have a group that is either listening to endless reports or trying to micro-manage the operational administration of the congregation. The future belongs to congregations that call and empower pastors who are leaders, and then also call and prepare governing boards that provide effective policy direction and leadership.

Sometimes congregations are reluctant to empower and support leadership because they are wary of leaders who may abuse and misuse their power. I know from past personal experiences and from the capacity of all of us for sin and self-deception that this is a reasonable concern. Therefore, it is important that pastoral leaders be subject to regular review and evaluation. It is also important, when leaders have responsibility for personnel supervision and actions, for there to be a grievance or appeal process. The elected governing body of a congregation does need to figure out ways to invite and receive congregational views on a consistent basis. Beyond that, the evaluation and review process for that governing body will normally consist of the nominations and elections process. In other words, if the group or individuals who make it up have functioned poorly, they should not be renominated or reelected. Furthermore, such boards and offices should have term limits. This is a classic and wise mechanism for guarding against the concentration and abuse of power.

While many members of congregations do express a legitimate concern about leaders who may misuse or abuse their powers (hence the necessity of the structures and accountability mentioned above), it is my experience that we are often not sufficiently aware of the other side of the coin. That is, congregations tend to be less aware of the importance of supporting and empowering effective leadership and of the cost of failing to do so. There is within many congregations, and even within whole denominations, an innate suspicion of leadership and power that strikes to the core of our systemic decline as denominations and congregations. It is my conviction that there is no one factor that is more central to the decline of mainline Protestant churches and denominations than the tendency in such bodies to devalue leadership, to be suspicious of those who would lead, and to attack or undermine those who do exercise leadership.

If leaders who abuse or misuse their powers have a cost — and they do — the frequent failure of churches to call forth, support, and empower faithful and capable leadership also has a cost, and it may be a far greater cost than we know. Too many who would and could be leaders today are undermined and undercut. The result is that congregations, rather than making progress and being faithful and effective, descend and decline into bodies that lack direction and are chronically conflicted. It doesn't have to be that way, and if there is to be hope for the future, it must not be that way.

Why Are We Here?

There is a legendary story from the waning years of the Student Christian Movement, a popular and productive movement for young Christians during the first half of the twentieth century and into the 1960s, particularly in Europe. In the early 1970s, SCM went belly up. A sign on the door of SCM's defunct central office in England famously read: "Gone out of business because we didn't know what business we were in." It happens. Organizations get spread so wide and thin that there is no longer a main channel. Institutions become so focused on the means that they forget and neglect the ends. Maintaining and enhancing the organization itself becomes the end rather than a means to an end or purpose. Groups try to do everything, and they end up accomplishing very little. Reasonable clarity about purpose is crucial to congregational vitality, especially in our new time. If a congregation doesn't know what business it is in, it may find itself, like the Student Christian Movement, hanging a "gone out of business" sign on the door.

Management guru Peter Drucker was well known for posing two simple but revealing questions to his clients: "What business are you in?" and "How's business?" Churches, church-related organizations, judicatories, and denominations would be well-advised to take these two questions seriously as well.[1] I recall posing a similar question to the members of a pastoral search committee during an interview: "What do

1. Peter Drucker, quoted in C. Kirk Hadaway, *Behold I Do a New Thing* (Cleveland: Pilgrim Press, 2001), p. 10.

you believe this church is trying to accomplish for God?" The question caught members of the committee by surprise and left them groping for words. One man, looking somewhat offended by the question, said, "Well, we're trying to do what we've always done, of course, the things that have made this church great." His response revealed a complete lack of clarity about purpose. I do not mean to suggest that easy, glib, or slogan-style answers are sufficient; I mean to say that vital congregations have a compelling, biblically shaped, theologically informed purpose or reason for being that marshals their energies and resources and directs their use.

A symptom that such a compelling shared purpose does not exist is the phenomenon referred to nowadays as "burnout," which seems to be everywhere. Many a minister and quite a few lay leaders and volunteers speak of burnout: "I've been to so many meetings, I'm just burned out." "It was such a long process and we never seemed to come to a conclusion — I'm just burned out." "It feels as if we as a congregation are burned out, exhausted, weary."

Ministry is certainly demanding, and congregational life is at times taxing. But I have come to believe that the word and phenomenon known as "burnout" are more symptomatic than accurately descriptive of what is going on for church leaders and congregations who use the term. It is not simply a matter of being overworked; it is often a lack of clarity about the nature of the work we are engaged in. "Burnout," the word and the lament, is symptomatic of the absence of a reasonably clear and compelling purpose. Lacking clear and compelling purpose, congregations (and clergy) tend to become reactive: they try to respond to every need, itch, hurt, and crisis that comes along. And *that* is a recipe for burnout, because people's needs, itches, and hurts are limitless and endless. Moreover, when there is a lack of shared purpose, congregations and clergy tend to become too focused on keeping everyone happy and together. Instead of being the captain and crew on the *Mayflower*, the vessel bound for a new world, the church begins to look more like the *Love Boat*, which goes nowhere but promises fun and entertainment for all! The worst thing that can happen on the *Love Boat* is for it to lose a member or several members, that is, to have unhappy passengers. But in a Christian congregation, losing a member or even a group of members is not, in truth, the end of the world; indeed, it may be a consequence, albeit a painful one, of reaching clarity about missional purpose.

I have noticed that church members often find serving on a pastoral search committee to be one of the most enjoyable and rewarding tasks they have performed in their church. This is not because it is easy: usually it entails long hours and serious, sustained effort, and it may include times of discouragement and disappointment. But there is a clear purpose: to identify our congregation's leadership needs and to find and call the right leader. That purpose is a compelling one, because most pastoral search committees understand that their work and selection will have significant consequences for their church. Moreover, it can be a spiritually transformational experience as the group comes to rely on the Spirit's guidance and finds itself changed in the course of its work. Along the way, members of such a committee usually have important conversations with one another, learn things about themselves, each other, and their church, and form relationships. In that process they may lose a member who realizes that he or she is not fully committed to the purpose of the group. While that is regrettable, others realize that the work — their shared purpose — is more important than any one person. All of these aspects of the search committee process make for an important and rewarding experience, but none of them would be sufficient without some success in achieving their reason for being — their purpose.

In our new time, many long-established congregations are overdue for a serious and informed conversation about church purpose. Why are we here? What business are we in? How's business? What is God calling us to be and to do? What is important to be doing in the next five years to more effectively fulfill our reason for being? Without reasonable clarity on such issues, congregations tend to undermine leaders, squander resources, and court frustration and burnout. With reasonable clarity of purpose, congregations are more likely to experience vitality and joy. As the old saw has it, "If you're not sure where you're trying to go, any route will do (and none of them will get you there)."

Congregations could do worse than adopting the slogan of a Seattle microbrewery: "The main thing is to keep the main thing the main thing." In this chapter I invite readers into a conversation about the "main thing": congregational purpose. After getting some clearer sense of our present context (Conversation 1), animating our sense of response-ability and urgency (Conversation 2), submitting ourselves for heart surgery (Conversation 3), and recognizing the crucial importance of leadership (Conversation 4), I want to focus this conversation on attaining reasonable clarity about purpose. With that in mind, we will look at the work of several church leaders and teachers who have helpfully engaged these central questions, and we'll investigate what key New Testament texts have to say about why we are here. My point in this chapter is not to tell you what your church's purpose should be. The point is to engage you and your congregation in this conversation and to encourage you to arrive at an articulation of a core purpose: a purpose that is your own, one that is reasonably clear, and one that is compelling.

Michael Foss and the Church as a Culture of Discipleship

In his several books, Michael Foss says that the great challenge facing many congregations today is to shift from a culture of membership to a culture of discipleship. To Foss, discipleship is the point: it is the purpose, the end, and the business churches are in. "We are long overdue," says Foss, "for a paradigm shift in American Protestantism — a shift from a membership model of church affiliation to a discipleship model." Foss describes the membership model by drawing on the analogy of the modern health club: "One becomes a member of the health club by paying dues (in a church, the monthly or weekly offering). Having paid their dues, the members expect the services of the club to be at their disposal: exercise equipment, weight room, aerobics classes, an indoor track, swimming pool — all there for them, with a trained staff to see that they benefit from them. Members may bring a guest on occasion, but only those who pay their dues have a right to the use of the facilities and the attention of the staff."[2]

The point is that, in the membership model or membership culture, purpose has devolved into meeting the needs of the members, into providing its members with goods and services that are called religious or spiritual. It is the job of the clergy, the staff, and a few lay leaders to produce something called "ministry" that will be used and consumed by the members. The church becomes a sort of a spiritual cul-de-sac, and

2. Michael W. Foss, *Power Surge: Six Marks of Discipleship for a Changing Church* (Minneapolis: Augsburg Fortress, 2000), p. 5.

congregation members thinks of themselves as "end-users" of God's grace. To put it another way, the membership model cuts the nerve of mission and turns the church into an organization that exists to serve those who are already there.

There is a pernicious secondary consequence of the focus on member satisfaction as the raison d'etre of a congregation: it creates a dynamic of inclusion and exclusion. "The membership model sets the church over against those outside the membership," says Foss. "The whole notion of the 'church for others' gets lost, and people act, both consciously and unconsciously, to protect the 'church for ourselves'" (*Power Surge*, p. 19). This misses the point, according to Foss, and distorts the church. The point is discipleship, "a spiritual transformation that leads to confident followership of Jesus Christ."[3]

My own epiphany regarding the prevalence and power of the membership model came as I listened to members of my own congregation introduce themselves to one another in a new group. The default pattern for introductions in the congregation was to give your name and say how long you had been a member of the church. Some useful information may be exchanged in the course of such an introduction, but something else is going on as well. A pecking order is being established. The longer someone has been a member of that church, the higher up in the pecking order she is and the more her views are to be taken as authoritative. This establishes who's in and who's out (or at least "less in"): that is, the membership culture has an inherently "insider-outsider" dynamic. This is one of the main distortions of faith that Jesus opposed.

I wondered what it would look like if members of a congregation were to learn a different default pattern for introducing themselves to one another when a new group, class, or task force gathered. Instead of saying how long we had been members of this congregation, we might give our names and share a few words about how it has been going for us lately as followers of Jesus — that is, as disciples. What has been rewarding in our discipleship journey, and what has been challenging? Such a shift would level the playing field of the church. While it is also certainly possible to abuse this format, it could overcome the "insider-outsider" pecking-order dynamics of the "member since" format. Those engaged in the conversation would be focused on something congruent

3. Foss, *Servant's Manual* (Minneapolis: Fortress, 2002), p. 2.

with the purpose of the church, namely, calling, forming, and sustaining disciples of Jesus Christ.

The shift from a culture of membership to a culture of discipleship has other implications as well. Often in the culture of membership there is an operative assumption that ordained ministers and the church staff are responsible for the spiritual life and health of that church's members. Pastors and preachers are supposed to get and keep people excited, entertained, and interested. If people lose interest in the church or Christian faith, it is the pastor's fault. In reality, however, each individual is responsible for his or her own spiritual journey and spiritual life, and all of us who are together in a congregation are responsible for the vitality, mission, and life of the congregation. Ordained clergy have a role in that, but it is a distortion to make them wholly responsible for the spiritual life of others. "The key to understanding the culture of a discipleship congregation," says Foss, "is found in the fact that those who accept the call to discipleship are committed to the personal practice of their own faith." To this end, Foss commends six "marks of discipleship": daily prayer, weekly worship, regular reading of the Bible, service to others, spiritual friendships, and generous giving. None of these marks of discipleship would be considered new or surprising, but Foss is clear that the purpose of the church is discipleship, and the means for growing disciples are these "marks," or practices. A shift occurs when we emphasize these "marks": clergy and staff give responsibility back to people in the congregation.[4]

Michael Foss makes a helpful contribution to our discussion of purpose by claiming that the purpose of the church is discipleship and the point is to call people to a way of life engaged in following Jesus Christ. While I am grateful for Foss's work and appreciative of his clarity, I would also note a few cautions. Though I don't think Foss falls into this temptation, it is possible in using these ideas and themes to become overly prescriptive. That is, we can fall into the error of saying, "This is precisely what a good disciple of Jesus does, looks like, thinks, and how he or she acts." Discipleship needs to be kept somewhat open-ended by the acknowledgment that there are many forms and expressions of faithful discipleship. It's not about fitting a mold; it is about following a living Lord.

4. Foss, *Power Surge,* p. 66.

Perhaps another way of saying this, and another caution, is that any list of marks, such as the one Foss proposes, can tempt us to turn our Christian faith into a project or performance. We can too easily turn daily prayer, service, or generous giving into something to be achieved, like weight loss or good grades or production quotas. We make our Christian faith and experience too much about what *we* do and not enough about what God does. While such marks can be helpful, we always need to remind ourselves that these are ways of responding to God's love and grace, not ways of earning that love.

Finally, the discipleship approach could become distorted if we emphasize individuals at the expense of the community of faith. That is, we could become so focused on our individual discipleship journey or experience, or the church's mission of making disciples, that we forget that the church as a group or body is also important. We are more than a collection of individual disciples. We are, or seek to be, the church, the people of God and the body of Christ.

No formulation of church purpose is without the possibility of distortion or misapplication, including Michael Foss's "culture of discipleship." But these cautions should be no more than that — cautions and reminders. Overall, the formulation of church purpose from this perspective and framework is powerful and potentially helpful. Why are we here? We are here to grow disciples of Jesus Christ. What business are we in? The business of helping people live a life of confident followership, and thus to participate in God's love in Jesus Christ for a broken and bruised world.

For Reflection and Discussion

• What do you think are the most important differences between a "membership culture" and a "discipleship culture"?

Kirk Hadaway and a Purpose-Based Church Typology

In his book *Behold I Do a New Thing*, sociologist of religion C. Kirk Hadaway uses a church typology that provides another helpful way to consider church purpose. Hadaway notes that the four types in the typology are models for learning and discussion and that no one congregation perfectly fits any one type. Perhaps more importantly by way of introduction, his typology assumes that the purpose of churches is a simple but powerful one: to change lives. Hadaway cites Peter Drucker's pithy observation: "The business of a church is to change people; the business of a corporation is to satisfy them."[5]

Hadaway himself acknowledges that this statement of purpose requires further elaboration. To say that the church exists to change lives says something very important; but it is not, at it stands, complete or sufficient. The concept of what the nature of this change will be needs to be developed. Nevertheless, the working hypothesis that a church exists to change lives enables Hadaway to develop what I have found to be a useful typology. Hadaway's typology enables us to investigate purpose and to see the ways in which purpose can be lost or displaced.

Hadaway also declares that purpose is more important than vision, and I agree with him. Vision is about where a group or congregation is going; purpose is about why we are here. Thus purpose precedes and shapes vision. Without a fairly clear sense of purpose, congregations can get caught up in the game of cultural catch-up or what's newest and latest. "A neighboring church is using video clips in the service and people like it. Let's try that." "A congregation in [a nearby city] has a rock band for its service, and lots of kids are coming. We should do that." "Their church is having huge success with its new Celtic Communion service." "At our denomination's convention, I heard about this neat program for outreach that's really working. Let's do it." These may or may not be good programs or strategies, but they usually raise the issue of purpose or ends. Why are we here? What are we trying to accomplish? The new strategies or programs set congregations and clergy on the spinning wheel of constantly implementing the latest hot innovation. It is better, Hadaway suggests, to be clear about why we are here and to work on being faithful to our purpose.

The four types of churches in Hadaway's typology are church as *club or clan,* church as *charismatic leader and followers,* church as *company or corporation,* and church as *incarnational community.*[6] The first two are types of churches that have "displaced" their purpose; the second two types have purpose "in place." Yet there is a crucial difference between the third and fourth types. The church as company or corpora-

---

5. Hadaway, *Behold I Do a New Thing,* p. 11.
6. Hadaway, *Behold I Do a New Thing,* pp. 49-65.

tion has predetermined outcomes in mind, while the church as incarnational community is more open-ended. Let's look at the four types briefly.

Hadaway notes that the vast majority of congregations in North America are small churches, usually under 200 members, often fewer than 100. While it is not necessarily true that small churches will fall into the club or clan type of church, many smaller congregations do tend in this direction. The church as club or clan might also be described as "a congenial community": it's like a family; however, also like a family, it tends to be hard to join. Those on the inside tend to have a strong sense of belonging and often speak of the congregation as "warm" and "caring." "This church is my family," would be a typical person's summing up of the relationship. At the same time, a newcomer or outsider may describe the same congregation as "cold" and "standoffish." And it's the same congregation! In the church as club or clan, people are known by name and there is a strong sense of community. These are good things, but the problem is that purpose has been displaced. Instead of changing lives, the purpose of the club or clan type of church has become the comfort and satisfaction of the congregation's members. So Hadaway's image for this type of church is the recliner chair.

Purpose has also been displaced in the church as charismatic leader and followers. There aren't nearly as many of these kinds of churches as there are club and clan congregations, but they do tend to be quite visible. Their services may be carried on television or radio, or their charismatic leader may be prominently featured on billboards, ads on buses, or in other promotions. Hadaway describes this kind of congregation as "a movement under command." The charismatic leader is in complete control. Such congregations tend toward boom and bust cycles, depending on the vitality of the charismatic leader. If she or he dies, or otherwise suffers a reversal of fortune, the ministry tends to go from boom to bust. While they are prominent, such congregations have also displaced their purpose from changing lives to meeting the needs of the charismatic leader. The church is not really a congregation so much as it is a collection of individuals who follow that person. Hadaway's image for the church as charismatic leader and followers is a guided missile. But he adds that the missile is often mis-aimed — that is, misguided!

The church as company or corporation and the church as incarnational community both have the purpose of changing lives in place, but the difference between the two is important. In the company or corporation church there are specific tangible goals and predetermined outcomes, while in the incarnational community church the goals are more diffuse, intangible, and open-ended. Hadaway argues that religious organizations and congregations that try to reduce their life to specific and tangible goals end up distorting the real church, where outcomes are necessarily more intangible and open-ended. When we turn the church into another organization driven by goals and objectives, we lose something.

Despite that, the church as company or corporation does have its purpose — changing lives — in place, and many such congregations do accomplish great good. For the most part, such congregations tend to be the larger Protestant and Roman Catholic congregations of North America. They are organizations with a plan and they "work the plan." This may result in impressive ministries of housing for the homeless, booming Sunday schools and Vacation Bible Schools, "meals-on-wheels" ministries, or similar programs, and they touch lives and change them. But sometimes, at least, the emphasis on measuring the ministry, on working the plan, means that such congregations are so busy doing things for God's world that they can forget to encounter or experience God. Furthermore, ministry programs tend to take on a life of their own: they may become sacred cows that cannot be changed or challenged, even though times and needs have changed. Hadaway's image for this type of church is a factory, a factory that molds its members.

The fourth type of church, the church as incarnational community, is not the opposite of the other three; in fact, it incorporates elements of each. There is, as in the church as club or clan, a sense of community and caring; like the church of the charismatic leader and followers, it has a sense of direction; like the church as company or corporation, it has purposeful action. But none of those three characteristics has become so predominant as to override everything else. Community, direction, and purposeful action all find their place in the incarnational community, but they do not become the purpose. The purpose is changing lives and being a church that incarnates, or embodies, its purpose, which is to be a community of transformation. Unlike the church as company or corporation, where the goals are set and predetermined, the incarnational community keeps its goals and actions more open. This is because one never knows precisely where God will lead or what

changes the Holy Spirit will bring about. Instead of pointing to numbers, as in the company or corporation church, incarnational community congregations will tell stories of lives changed, stories of God's
working in people's lives and in the community.

As Hadaway notes, and as I observed in introducing his typology,
these are types and abstractions. Reality is more complicated. Many
congregations exhibit characteristics of more than one type. Nevertheless, this typology can serve a useful purpose in evoking discussion of
questions such as "Why are we here?" and "What business are we in?"
Have we lost or displaced our purpose in favor of keeping members
comfortable and satisfied? Is our real purpose to meet the needs of a
powerful and persuasive leader? Have we, at least sometimes, reduced
our church to projects and activities to be accomplished rather than en-
counters with the mysterious and powerful Lord of life, who upsets our
systems and disturbs our plans?

In the balance of his book, Hadaway further develops the simple
statement of purpose that undergirds his typology: that the purpose of
churches is to change lives.[7] While he avoids becoming overly prescriptive, he does indicate that churches exist to grow people of faith and help
people live in God's kingdom as proclaimed and embodied by Jesus, and
that incarnational communities support and sustain lives of discipleship. Hadaway's image for the fourth church type is an aspen grove. This
kind of church is an organic, growing system: individuals are nurtured
by the community, and the individuals, in turn, bring their gifts to the
larger community. An incarnational community is not organized or run
like a factory or corporation; it is tended like a garden. There is a "magi-
cal" element, a transforming power at work, that we humans do not control and cannot bend to our will. We can bring the right ingredients; but
when they are mixed together, something happens that we cannot control or predict. However, we can be open to the mysterious power of life,
change, healing, and transformation that is God's.

As I did with Foss's culture of discipleship, I will add a few cautions
about Kirk Hadaway's very helpful typology. "Changing lives" can also
become distorted by our own agendas and egos. We contemporary
Americans tend to want instant change, and we often want change that
will make us look or feel better. The changes wrought by God's grace in

---

7. Hadaway, *Behold I Do a New Thing*, pp. 49-75.

Jesus Christ tend not to be instant, and they will, in all likelihood, lead us away from a preoccupation with ourselves. Too many contemporary testimonies for Jesus sound like testimonies for another life-enhancing product or service rather than the gospel call to lose one's life for Jesus' sake and the sake of the gospel.

A second caution is similar to one I expressed about Foss's work: the approach could become overly individualistic and forget that, while God does seek to change individual lives, God also seeks to create a people. The church, the community of faith that is blessed to be a blessing, is part of God's purpose and should not be eclipsed by an emphasis on transforming or changing individuals. Of course, the two go together, and they should not be pulled apart.

Hadaway's typology, with those caveats, provides a very helpful device for exploring the question of purpose. It reveals some of the subtle ways that purpose can be lost or displaced, often not in the service of obviously "bad" things but in the service of good ones: being a caring and comfortable community, having strong leadership, or accomplishing goals. One additional attractive aspect of Hadaway's typology is that it does not give preference to the large church or assume that, just because there are a lot of people there, a church is being faithful to its purpose. Often smaller congregations of the club or clan type have the idea that someday they will grow up and become a real church, by which they usually mean a church that is of the company or corporation type. Until then they say, "Well, we're just a small church — you can't expect too much." If, as Hadaway claims, the purpose of the church is to change lives and grow people of faith, the small-membership congregation that is clear about its purpose is as capable of fulfilling that purpose as the large-membership church is. There is no need to "grow up and become a real church." Smaller congregations in which lives are being changed, where people are truly growing in faith and the life of faith, are real churches — regardless of size.

For Reflection and Discussion

- How do you respond to Hadaway's claim that purpose ("why are we here?") is more important than vision ("where are we going?")?
- Remembering that no one congregation perfectly fits any of the types in Hadaway's typology, which type or types best describe your congregation?

Diana Butler Bass and Intentional Congregations

As the twenty-first century began, Diana Butler Bass, historian of American religion and a student of contemporary congregational life, noticed something that both the mainstream media and other scholars seemed to miss. There was new vitality in the old mainline. The denominations that historically descended from the Protestant Reformation and had been in a period of decline were showing, here and there, signs of new life. Congregations of the old mainline — not all, but some — were newly vital. Bass noticed something else: that these newly vital congregations were congregations of what she called "intentional practice." By this she meant that these vital churches were discovering or re-discovering ancient spiritual practices as ways of forming Christian identity and furthering mission. Such practices included discernment, hospitality, prayer and meditation, lectio divina (a way of reading the Bible), Sabbath-keeping, catechesis, and more. Bass set out to study these congregations of intentional practice: her study was called "The Project on Congregations of Intentional Practice," and the first book (of several) to report her findings was entitled *The Practicing Congregation: Imagining a New Old Church.*[8]

In *The Practicing Congregation,* Bass develops a distinction that is germane to our discussion of purpose: the distinction between "established churchgoing" and "intentional churchgoing." Congregations in Bass's study that were exhibiting signs of new life and vitality had changed from established churchgoing to intentional churchgoing. Before going into these two categories further, however, I want to note Bass's own observation that American religion has been commonly explained in terms of the two-party system: the distinction between liberal and conservative churches. While this distinction has some descriptive value and basis in history, Bass claims that it is not particularly helpful or accurate for those wishing to understand what is happening with congregations in North America today. Simply lumping them into groups called "liberal" or "conservative" does not tell us much, partly because most congregations include a range of people along such a spectrum, and partly because the categories themselves reflect an ear-

8. Diana Butler Bass, *The Practicing Congregation: Imagining a New Old Church* (Herndon, VA: Alban Institute, 2004), pp. 82-84.

lier era, the period of modernity. In our postmodern era the liberal-conservative polarity may generate a good deal of heat, but not much light. Bass suggests that a more useful explanatory device, one that cuts across the liberal-conservative duality, is to look at congregations along a spectrum of "established" to "intentional." As we look at these two categories, keep in mind the question of purpose and the implied purposes of each of Bass's types.

Established churchgoing, according to Bass, characterizes the mainline Protestant establishment and the time in North America when such congregations were the religious establishment of the culture. Going to church, being members of some congregation — this was what one did. Bass also refers to this as "accidental churchgoing": by this she means that you had not really chosen it and you didn't think much about it. You simply went to this or that church because your parents did or your grandparents did. Or maybe you didn't go (except on Christmas and Easter) but nonetheless said, "That's my church (that I don't attend)." "Accidental churchgoing," says Bass,

> was the pattern of the mainline Protestant establishment — a style of religious practice that dominated religion for much of the twentieth century. Established Protestantism was marked by its chapel orientation. Church was a place to go where a minister performed certain spiritual tasks for the congregants (who usually inherited the faith from parents). Chapel religion typically blesses the social order, comforts people in times of crisis, and trains children in the customs of faith. . . . Chapel-style churches are routinized organizations, where members *receive* customs, traditions, and beliefs rather than create new ones.[9]

As you read this description, recall the discussion of American Christendom in the first conversation. Bass is describing, in slightly different words, the church of that era and its role and purposes. It blessed the social order, provided comfort amid crisis, and trained children in religious customs.

As the twentieth century waned, a new kind of church and orientation toward participation in congregational life began to emerge: it reflected the new era's emphasis on choice, mobility, reflection, self-

9. Bass, *Practicing Congregation*, p. 78.

awareness, and spirituality. Instead of assuming or inheriting a given religious identity, with its chapel-style experience, intentional church-going tended to be more demanding.

> Intentional congregations . . . think about what they do and why they do it in relation to their own history, their cultural context, the larger Christian story found in scripture and liturgy, and in line with the longer traditions of Christian faith. In addition to thinking about their practices, they reflexively engage practices that best foster their sense of identity and mission.[10]

In words that are reminiscent of Michael Foss's distinction between membership culture and discipleship culture, Bass says:

> The accidental practices of established churchgoing assume insider status (the parishioner, or his or her family, has been part of the community for a long time) and often display low-demand characteristics in terms of spiritual rigor. The minister, a paid professional, typically performs religious tasks on behalf of the community. In contrast, intentional practices assume nothing about status — and they cost something in terms of choice, commitment, and involvement. In intentional congregations, this costliness creates a palpable sense of communal discipleship, mentoring, mutual learning, and spiritual formation; a pilgrim sensibility of people traveling together in community, whose practices embody a particular way of life in the world.[11]

If purpose in the established churchgoing congregation can be described as blessing the social order, providing comfort amid crisis, and training children in religious customs, the focus and purpose are different in intentional churchgoing congregations. The purpose is suggested in the final sentence of the Bass quotation: "To embody a particular way of life in the world." Practices serve to support this particular way of life as well as to embody and express it. The purpose is similar to that of Foss, a culture of discipleship, and to that of Hadaway, to change lives and grow people of faith.

10. Bass, *Practicing Congregation*, p. 80.
11. Bass, *Practicing Congregation*, p. 81.

As is true of Hadaway's typology, Bass's portraits of established and intentional churchgoing tend toward ideal types, whereas reality may be more messy and mixed. That's why she speaks of these not as two distinct categories but as a spectrum. Congregations and individuals will probably locate themselves somewhere along the spectrum between established and intentional rather than simply saying, "We are this, not that." Still, the descriptions are revealing and point to both a changing purpose for the church and changes in the church's cultural context that permit and require such change. The intentional congregation takes as its purpose to form people of faith, people who participate in a particular way of life identified as "Christian": this is, if not at odds with the prevailing values and norms of the larger North American society, at least in tension with them. In pointing to congregations of intentional churchgoing, Bass contributes significantly to our discussion of purpose. She does so, in part, by helping us see how the cultural context of the church's life and ministry has changed, and helping us see that, as one hymn puts it, "New occasions teach new duties, time makes ancient good uncouth." In this new time, congregations teach and embody a particular way of life.

For Reflection and Discussion
- Reflect on your own faith journey. Would you characterize it as established or intentional — or both?

Church Purpose and Scripture

We are not, of course, left to contemporary teachers and interpreters alone, however helpful their work may be. We have the Old and New Testaments to guide us. Before the purpose of the church was the purpose of God's people, Israel. That purpose is succinctly stated in Genesis 12:2, the call to Abraham. "I will bless you . . . so that you will be a blessing." Israel and the New Israel, the church, are those who have known the blessing of God and who are called to be a blessing to all the peoples of the earth. We are receivers of grace who are called to be instruments of grace on behalf of the world God created and loves. Recall the story of the seminary student who spoke of people in the church she served as having had no experience of the blessing of the gospel but were still trying to do mission. The blessing of God is the source of the church's mission to be a blessing.

In the Gospel of Matthew, the purpose of the church is encapsulated in the charge Jesus gave to his disciples in the final verses of that Gospel: "Go therefore and make disciples of all nations [a word that should be understood as "peoples"], baptizing them in the name of the Father and of the Son and of the Holy Spirit, and teaching them to obey everything that I have commanded you. And remember that I am with you always, to the end of the age" (Matt. 28:19-20). The emphasis here falls clearly on making disciples, students of the teacher, followers of the Master. And in what might be considered an inversion of the "blessed to be a blessing" pattern of Genesis, here the promise, "Lo, I am with you always," is predicated on the "Go therefore and make disciples." As one preacher memorably put it, "If there ain't no 'Go,' then there ain't no 'Lo'!" The club or clan type of church and the membership culture church have largely forgotten the "Go."

In the Gospel of John, when Jesus came to his frightened disciples after the crucifixion and resurrection, he gave them a similar charge: "As the Father has sent me, so I send you" (John 20:21). Prior to this charge, this sending into the world, Jesus had breathed the Holy Spirit into them and pronounced God's peace on them. But this peace is not a separate peace that is apart from the world: it is a peace that sends those who have known the blessing of Christ into the world. Earlier, in the Gospel of John's farewell discourse, Jesus had said to the disciples: "I tell you, the one who believes in me will also do the works that I do and, in fact, will do greater works than these, because I am going to the Father" (John 14:12). The disciples are sent into the world to speak the words and do the works that Jesus did, to continue his mission of being a light for the world.

The church's purpose and mission are also succinctly stated in the first chapter of Acts: "But you will receive power when the Holy Spirit has come upon you; and you will be my witnesses in Jerusalem, in all Judea and Samaria, and to the ends of the earth." The church is called to be a Spirit-led and -empowered witness to what God has done and to the risen Lord. Here, as in all these texts, mission is not one aspect or program or line item within the church's overall life. The church is itself mission: its purpose in its entire life is to be a missional outpost of God's kingdom and of the new creation.

A somewhat different kind of purpose statement may be drawn from the Gospel of Mark. When Jesus is asked to sum up the law and God's intent in response to the question about which of the commandments is "the greatest," he answers: "You shall love the Lord your God with all your heart, and with all your soul, and with all your mind, and with all your strength," and "you shall love your neighbor as yourself" (Mark 12:30). The love of God and the love of neighbor are a powerful summation of the purpose of life and the purpose of the faithful.

We could draw on other passages and texts of Scripture beyond these examples. The meaning of "making disciples," "being sent into the world," and being "my witnesses" can and should be further explored and explicated. Yet this much is clear: the church does not need to invent its reason for being, nor have we been left clueless. Many are the clues and directions for congregations that wish to think clearly and act resolutely concerning purpose.

For Reflection and Discussion
- Of the various biblical passages cited — Genesis, Matthew, John, Acts, and Mark — which speaks most powerfully to you?
- What implications do you see for centering your congregation's life in one or more of these purpose statements from Scripture?

Purpose: Concluding Reflections

Why are we here? What business are we in? How's business? These are important questions for congregations and their leaders in our new time. We can no longer assume that the purposes that animated the church in the time of American Christendom and modernity are as compelling or adequate as they were then. As I indicated in the introduction to this conversation, it is not my intention to prescribe what your church's purpose is or should be. But it is my intention to express how crucial it is for congregations to engage in serious conversation about purpose and these questions. Moreover, I urge congregations that are seeking to be vital in our new time to gain the capacity to articulate their purpose and to build their life together around a reasonably clear and compelling articulation of purpose.

Thus far we have several different articulations of purpose. Michael

Foss has given us a statement of purpose that correlates with his discussion of the church as a culture of discipleship. The point is discipleship, confident following of Jesus Christ and participation in God's love for the world. Kirk Hadaway offers the succinct statement that churches exist to change lives, as well as the somewhat more elaborate statement that the purpose of the church is to grow people of faith. And we can draw from Diana Butler Bass and her concept of intentional church-going the idea that churches exist to form and sustain people in a particular way and practice of life, the Christian way of life. We can hear other purpose statements in Scripture: the church is a people who have been blessed by God to be a blessing to others, "making disciples" and "being [Christ's] witnesses," among others.

Before concluding this conversation, I would like to suggest one additional way to frame congregational purpose. This one reaches a little further back into the Christian tradition, back to the seventeenth century and the Westminster Shorter Catechism, which begins with the following question and answer: "Question: What is the chief end of man? Answer: The chief end of man is to glorify God and enjoy him forever." (The antiquated word "man" is, of course, a generic term for human beings.) This statement of why we are here seems to me both compelling and helpful for congregations trying to reclaim a vivid sense of purpose. Our purpose is to direct women and men, youth and children, and all of life toward its creator, toward God, the God revealed in Jesus Christ. Our lives — and life in general — are pointed toward this end: to glorify God and to enjoy God. We do not live for ourselves, or as the apostle Paul put it, "unto ourselves alone."

This means that worship, as a particular activity or practice of the church of all ages, is especially central and important. But it means more. It means that, while worship is an end in itself, it is also training or formation in the very purpose of life. In worship we orient and reorient our lives toward God, the Father, Son, and Holy Spirit. We seek to be and become people and communities that live God-centered (or *theo-centric*) lives. Given our natural yet sinful propensity for centering life around ourselves, as well as for being distracted by many things, this is no mean undertaking. It requires work and energy. Thus liturgy may be defined (from the Greek *leitourgia*) as "the work of the people," or "people's energy." But this formulation of purpose posits that we human beings are, by our true nature, worshiping creatures, creatures who find our fullest realization not simply in daily work or family or marriage or nation and citizenship, as important as any of those relationships may be, but in relationship to God and as creatures who glorify God in all that we do and are. Such is our purpose, and that is one statement of it.

Even as we consider other more contemporary statements of the purpose of the church — "to make disciples," "to grow people of faith," "to practice a Christian way of life," as well as biblical statements of purpose — let us not forget this wonderful old statement of our chief end or purpose: "To glorify God and enjoy God forever." I close with this statement of purpose because it reminds us that the purpose of the church is not, in the end, something we achieve or produce. Rather, purpose means our attempt to conform our lives to their true nature and calling, to our true end and purpose, to put God at the center of our lives because God is our center, our source, and our destiny.

Congregations today need to be reasonably clear about their purpose, and they need to articulate it consistently and winsomely. But simply writing a mission or purpose statement should not deceive us. Writing or stating purpose is one thing, but living it and making it real is another. Congregations often have a pretty decent mission statement, or if they are pushed, will come up with purpose statements similar to those we have considered. That's necessary, but not sufficient. From there congregations and their leaders need to go forward and take such statements seriously, letting them guide, encourage, and discipline the life of the congregation. Some churches do have great purpose or mission statements, but those statements stay on the shelf, in the report, on the T-shirt or banner, and they do not get translated into congregational life, ministry, decision-making, resource allocation, and priority-setting. Lesser or different purposes, like some of Hadaway's "displaced purposes," hold sway. A reasonably clear and compelling statement of purpose is important, but making it real is also essential. To this issue of "making it real" we now turn in our next conversation.

Write the Vision

Let's remind ourselves of the flow of the conversation we have been having. In the first conversation, "It's Not about You," we discussed major shifts in the culture of North America and how those impact congregations. Neither you nor I made these huge cultural shifts happen, and thus the title of that conversation. Our next conversation turned the tables: "It *Is* about You." Although we didn't bring about these tectonic shifts in our culture, how you and I and our congregations respond to the challenges and opportunities of this new time is the real issue. Our third conversation, "A New Heart," took the notion that it *is* about us further, claiming that a fresh turning, a renewing of hearts and minds, is more important than any technique or program. "Who Shall Lead Them?" asks and tries to answer the question of leadership at several levels, all the while affirming that leadership's work is to help congregations face their own most important challenges and make progress on them. Then, in the just preceding conversation, the fifth, we explored the question of purpose: "Why Are We Here?" Reasonable clarity about our core purpose as church is essential to our having new vitality in our new time. That's where we have been.

Now let's take a look in the other direction: where we are going in our next five conversations. In the second conversation I introduced the concept of "adaptive challenges" from Ron Heifetz's conceptual work. Our next three conversations focus on key adaptive challenges that face most mainline congregations. In this sixth conversation, "Write the Vision," I want to discuss the relationship between "purpose" (Conversation 5) and "vision." I suggest that a congregation's vision is composed of several key adaptive challenges that flow from its purpose, and in this chapter I wish to focus first on the actual process of writing the vision. How does a congregation identify its key challenges and put them into a vision statement, or a strategic plan? Then, to illustrate how to "do the work," I will focus on two adaptive challenges as case studies in this chapter: "Stewardship as a Spiritual Practice" and "Deepening Adult Christian Formation." The discussion of these two adaptive challenges has a twofold goal: I want to illustrate the concept of "doing adaptive work," and these are the two crucial areas of work for most mainline congregations.

In the seventh and eighth conversations, I continue to focus on key adaptive challenges facing many congregations in this new time. The seventh conversation, "Let's Get (Less) Organized," is about how congregations are organized and structured. Broadly speaking, many congregations are working with organizational structures that don't work very well because they were designed for the era of Christendom. Furthermore, they were designed for maintenance, not mission. We turn in the eighth conversation to another crucial piece of adaptive work facing mainline congregations: "The Church and the Public Square." Most mainline Protestant congregations have been public churches, practicing civic engagement in a host of ways. Our eighth conversation focuses on that legacy and the shape that such engagement might take in this new time. In a very real sense, then, these next three conversations are focused on key adaptive challenges that historically mainline Protestant congregations encounter today. This is not to say that these are the only pieces of adaptive work that need to be done, or even that they are *your* pieces of adaptive work. They are simply adaptive challenges that face many churches, and discussing them will illustrate some of the principles of both doing and leading adaptive work.

To complete this midpoint pause and view ahead, our ninth conversation is called "Death and Resurrection." In some situations renewal is possible, but not in all. Sometimes a death — or something that looks and feels very much like death — is necessary for a resurrection to be possible. I will discuss two quite different cases of congregational death and resurrection in the ninth conversation. The final conversation is entitled "Where Do We Start?" Now that you have taken part in these nine particular conversations, what's the next step where you are?

Where do *you* begin? As the question is framed in Acts 2, "What, then, shall we do?" I hope that this look backward and forward has helped us get our bearings. As a way of checking, let's take a moment for reflection and discussion.

For Reflection and Discussion

- Of the five conversations that have begun this book, which one did you find most compelling? Why?
- In the next three chapters we will be talking about adaptive work in four areas: stewardship, adult Christian formation, church structure and governance, and civic engagement and public witness. Which of these is most urgent or exciting for you?

The Relationship of Purpose and Vision

On more than one occasion I have taken part in congregational or denominational gatherings where things were tense and people were frustrated with those in leadership. Often at such times, someone has gotten to his or her feet and said, with some degree of anger or frustration, "What's the vision? Tell us where we're going." It's a good question, but sometimes not the right question. We have become enamored of vision: we speak of the "vision thing," and we imagine leaders as those who "cast the vision." My contention is that "where we are headed," or vision, is secondary to "why we are here," our core reason for being, our *purpose.* Before we can meaningfully take on the question "What's the vision?" we have to have a reasonably clear, compelling, and shared notion of why we are here, or what our core purpose is. Vision, as I understand it and use it here, is made up of the pieces of work that are before us *in order* to further and more fully realize our purpose. Without clarity about our core purpose, vision tends to become a wish list, even a fantasy list of all our bright ideas, dreams, and hopes. With purpose in place, vision is made up of the next steps that God calls us to take in order to fulfill our purpose. Coming up with ideas that are appealing, that may even sound wonderful, is not that difficult. What is difficult, but crucially important, is being fairly clear about our purpose and staying on purpose. Another way to put this is to say that vision must be "strategic," which means that vision is related to purpose, that vision advances core purpose.

Frequently, when I have been invited to speak to a congregation or a denominational group about our new time, the end of Christendom and the waning of modernity, someone will come up after I have spoken and say, "Well, I guess we have to change." It often sounds as though the next (unspoken) sentence is, "But we're not going to (or *I'm* not going to)." I often respond: "No, I don't want you to change. I want you to stay the same." That person is, of course, taken aback. I continue: "I don't want you to change. I want you to figure out your purpose and then stay the same. I want you to stay on purpose. I want you to stay on your purpose like a dog on a bone." Of course, what I haven't said is that figuring out and living out the purpose — and doing so in ways formed by Scripture and informed by theology — may entail a good deal of change! But the point stands: we can become fixated on the notion of change. We figure that if we make changes like a church down the street or across town did, then we will have lots of people becoming new members, just as those congregations do. But then we are caught up in the same relentless cycles of the fashion world. We look for what's new, what's in, what's now. And usually by the time we pick it up, it's passé!

It is far better, I believe, to get reasonably clear about a compelling and biblically and theologically sound purpose. Different congregations will state or frame their purpose in different ways and words: "to grow in faith"; "to be and to make disciples of Jesus Christ"; "to grow people of faith who participate in God's work in the world"; "to be a community where Spirit and service meet"; "to know and love God, to know and love ourselves, to know and love others"; "to welcome all people with grace, as God has welcomed us." These are some of the purpose statements formulated by congregations with whom I have worked. The point is not that there is one perfect statement of purpose, but that vital congregations know what their purpose is and that it resonates with the core affirmations of Scripture and Christian conviction. The task is not to change, but to stay the same — to stay on purpose. But if we are to stay on purpose and more fully and faithfully realize and fulfill our purpose, it is likely that some change, learning, and growth will be required of us. That is where vision comes in. Given our purpose, our God-given reason for being, vision is about this question: "What is God calling us to do in the next one, three, five, or ten years so that we may more fully realize our purpose?"

Writing the Vision

Before we turn to the actual writing of the vision, let me briefly remind you of a key concept and distinction that I discussed in our second conversation, the distinction between technical problems and adaptive challenges. A technical problem is a problem that is known and that we can identify clearly: "too little space in the nursery" or "a Sunday school curriculum that is not accessible for our teachers." The solution is likewise clear and known: it involves the application of existing techniques. We break the nursery out into two rooms, or we knock out a wall and enlarge the existing nursery. We put together a team to review three or four Sunday school curricula and choose one they like best. Who does the work? Experts and authorities: people we pay, designate, or call to get the job done on our behalf.

Adaptive challenges are different. Initially, we may not even know quite how to name the challenge before us. We may want to call it "aging congregation" or "we need new members," but those may not be accurate descriptions or identifications of the challenge. Perhaps, with time, we come to name the challenge as "discovering again God's purpose for our church." Doing that work may involve some techniques we already know, but it will also involve taking risks and engaging in new behaviors. It will include learning and change. We may find ourselves talking with people we don't normally talk with; we may call on God and other people for help and insight; we may, like the disciples before Pentecost, need to wait for a word from the Lord. Who does the work? Not experts or authorities. Not the pastor, or a consultant, or a small group we designate to solve our problems for us. No, it is the people with the problem themselves, the people facing the challenge, who do the work. If the work is "discovering again God's purpose (mission) for our church," we can't simply assign that to a mission committee. Most everyone in the congregation must engage in this work in some form, because the real work is the changing of our hearts and our minds.

I review the distinction between technical problems and adaptive work because congregations often try to turn adaptive challenges into technical problems. For example, I mentioned the congregation with which I worked that was concerned that their percentage of worship attendance to membership was too low. It was about 20 percent. That is, on any given Sunday, only one in five church members took part in worship. Their solution was to add a new contemporary worship service with praise music and big screens. The new service would take place in the fellowship hall and be less formal. Who would do the work? The worship board, the pastors, and the musicians who would be hired. This solution treated the problem as largely a technical matter. I suggested that it might be looked at as an adaptive challenge. Perhaps, during the era of American Christendom, coming to worship only occasionally was enough. But if the purpose of the church is "to be and to make disciples of Jesus Christ," occasional attendance at worship won't do. "It could be," I suggested, "that you need to rethink your purpose and begin to consider changing the culture of your congregation. Apparently, the present culture of your congregation regards worship as optional. You've taught people that membership is more important than participation. I wonder how you might go about changing that. Who would have to learn what in order for that to change?"

Adding the contemporary service may prove to be a good strategy, or it may not. I don't know. But I do know that the issues before this congregation are deeper than a technical fix. It's not simply a matter of giving the existing congregation more choices. It is about the purpose of the church. It is about the members of the congregation engaging in learning and change, gaining new hearts and new minds as their expectations about church and being Christians are changed and their faith is deepened. We are facing adaptive challenges in the mainline Protestant churches. To the extent that we construe what is before us as technical problems only, we will fail. Moreover, we will have missed important, God-given opportunities to experience new hearts and minds.

I should note, however, that most congregations face a combination of technical problems and adaptive challenges. Or, to put it another way, the technical and the adaptive often come bundled: that is, there is a technical aspect to the work before us, but there is also an adaptive dimension. In the congregation cited above, doing the set-up work for a technically effective contemporary service may be part of the work. But the adaptive dimension will involve forming new expectations that begin to help people see that weekly participation in vital worship is essential to Christian life and faith and to being church together.

The point of this brief review of the technical problem and adaptive challenge distinction is that, when it comes to "Writing the Vision," most of what goes into the vision — that is, what God is calling us to do in the next one, three, five, or ten years — will be adaptive work that is before us as we seek to more fully realize and fulfill our purpose as a congregation. Therefore, the two "cases" I will discuss in this chapter, "Stewardship as a Spiritual Practice" and "Deepening Adult Christian Formation," are both, to my mind, adaptive challenges; and so are the topics of conversation in the following two chapters, "Let's Get (Less) Organized" and "The Church and the Public Square." Experts or authorities may have a part to play, but if we are going to make progress, it will be because a significant portion of the congregation is engaged in life-changing, faith-forming work.

Perhaps it will be helpful to give an example of what I mean by a vision plan or statement. Here's one:

Purpose: "To Grow People of Faith Who Participate in God's Work in the World."

Vision: In the next five years we have three priorities to more fully realize our purpose:

1. We believe that God is calling us to do serious leadership development work among lay members of our church in order for us to have a strong core of spiritually formed persons with leadership gifts, potential, and experience.
2. We believe that God is calling us to make a shift from the mentality of paying dues/taking a collection to learning the deeper meaning of offering and stewardship as the spiritual practice of growing in generosity.
3. We believe that God has called us to deepen our practice of adult Christian faith formation in order to help both those who are new to this church and those who have been involved for some time to grow in their faith.

If this were an actual vision plan, each of these three priorities would be developed with specific strategies for making progress on that particular priority. In developing strategies, we may find it helpful to use the acronym SMART as a guideline: it stands for *specific, measurable, actionable, realistic,* and having a *timeline.*

In summary, such a vision plan has three levels: *purpose* ("Why are we here?"); and then *vision* ("Given our purpose, what is God calling us to do in the next period of time [you determine your timelines]?"); and then *strategies,* which are more specific steps toward making progress on the particular priority that is part of the vision. I should express one caveat: such a vision plan is a plan, not an order or commandment or recipe. In other words, as we do the work and learn together, we may discover that we will need to make adjustments to our plan. The Spirit will move in ways we did not anticipate. A vision plan is a guideline to be taken seriously, but we will need to stay open and responsive to what God is doing in our midst, and open to new learning as we go.

Before we move on to the two case studies, there are three more questions that need to be discussed concerning writing the vision: *Who* writes the vision? *How* is the vision written? *What* is the process for coming up with a congregation's vision statement? These are important questions, and there is no one right answer to any of them. How this is done depends on a number of factors and variables: the history and style of your particular congregation, its denominational identity and polity, the congregation's governance structure, and the leadership style of the pastor and other staff persons.

Acknowledging that there is no single right way to come up with the vision statement or plan, I will offer one model for doing this work; I will suggest several qualities or characteristics to keep in mind as we do the work; and I will list a couple of resources that you can turn to if you choose.

Here's a model I have used. Start with your governing body, be it a church council, session, consistory, or whatever you call it. Introduce and establish the idea that periodic, purpose-based strategic planning is one of the responsibilities of this governing body. To fulfill that responsibility, the governing body may itself choose to lead the planning/vision-writing process, or they may choose to appoint another group, for example, "The Strategic Planning Team," or "Futures Team," or the "Write the Vision Group" to do the work on their behalf. Generally, it seems to work better when the governing body appoints a specific group to do the work on their behalf. If the governing body chooses that path, it should take time to carefully create the charge for that group, including specifying a timeline and specifying the ways to ensure ongoing communication between the governing body and the planning team.

The planning team is responsible for devising a process that brings a vision plan back to the governing body and then to the congregation within the agreed-on time (three to six months). That process should begin by their reviewing the last plan or vision statement and evaluating how that work went. The planning team next comes up with various ways by which members of the congregation have a voice and input. It's probably best to have several modes to get that done: open gatherings for conversation and discernment, written questionnaires, suggestion boxes, and so forth. All of this is done as discernment, that is, by asking, "Given our purpose, what do you sense God is calling us to do in the future to advance our purpose?" If discernment is new to the church, the planning team will need to spend some time learning the practice of discernment, drawing on resources listed below. In the end, the vision statement should reflect the contributions of (1) the congregation, (2) the governing board, (3) the pastor and/or pastoral staff, (4) analysis of the external environment (the larger community in which the church exists), and (5) an outside perspective. The outside perspective can be gained in several ways: engaging a consultant, involving a member of the denominational staff, or using the pastor or key leader from another church in the community. The point is to get an external viewpoint.

Key questions should be developed by the planning team for each of these five. After eliciting input, the planning team takes the contributions of all five segments and asks: "What is God calling us to focus on in the next period of time in order to more fully and faithfully realize our purpose as a church?" The planning team should come up with a short list of three to five major priorities, and then it should report back to the governing body and congregation. When the governing body and congregation have had a chance to hear their initial report, the planning team moves to the strategy level: developing strategies for each priority and then taking these back to the governing body, the pastoral staff, outside consultants, and the congregation for review and comment.

My experience is that doing this process every five years has been useful, but different congregations may find a different time frame a better fit. Once the governing board and congregation become accustomed to doing this work periodically, it will become an accepted practice. One benefit of doing such planning regularly is that not everything has to be in the plan in a particular five-year cycle (or if you choose a different time frame, three- or ten-year cycle). Some things rise to the top now, other things later. Having such a plan helps to build support and a sense of direction, determine allocation of human and financial resources, including pastoral and staff resources, and it provides a governing board with a basis for evaluation.

Whatever format you decide on to write the vision, here are some things to keep in mind: (1) The process builds on and is driven by your church purpose. (2) This is a discernment process: that is, the question is not "What do I or my group want?" but "What is God calling us to do at this time, given our purpose as a church?" (3) Make it very clear that you want and value everyone's participation; you value input, and everyone "has a place at the table." (4) Make the process clear from the get-go, including specifying who, in the end, will approve the vision plan. That could be the congregation or the elected governing body. Be clear which it is. (5) Keep information and communication flowing. The planning team should share frequent reports with the governing body and congregation and use different formats for doing so. For example, use the church newsletter, display boards and posters around the church building, the church website, and podcasts. (6) Stay positive, thanking people for their ideas and participation. (7) Remember that planning is planning, doing is doing.

Sometimes the planning process becomes so elaborate and time-consuming that we never get on to the doing. I suggest this planning work unfold over a brisk three- to six-month period. After the plan is in place, it is the responsibility of the governing body and those it designates to move ahead with the work. It is also up to the governing group and the key leaders, especially the pastor, to keep the purpose and vision before the congregation. The most common mistakes or failure points in the process are that planning becomes an end in itself, which means that there is no energy left when the planning is finished; or, second, once the planning is done, the vision loses visibility and is forgotten. Write the vision and make the plan. Wear the vision. Refer to it. Celebrate successes. Be a cheerleader. And most all, follow through! Congregations and their leaders must learn, in Heifetz's words, "to maintain disciplined attention."[1]

---

1. Let me suggest several resources that congregations and their leaders could use. On "discernment," see Danny E. Morris and Charles M. Olsen, *Discerning God's Will Together: A Spiritual Practice for the Church* (Herndon, VA: Alban Institute, 1997); see also Martin Copenhaver, *Decision-Making and Discernment for Vital Congregations* (Cleveland: Pilgrim Press, forthcoming). There are a number of resources on "planning," including Roy M. Oswald and Robert E. Friedrich Jr., *Discerning Your Congregation's Fu-*

For Reflection and Discussion
- Of the seven points in the last paragraph, which one(s) strike you as most relevant for your congregation?
- Try to put my distinction between *purpose* and *vision* in your own words.

Stewardship as a Spiritual Practice

Okay, let's say that your purpose is "growing people of faith," and that a key priority of your vision plan is "discovering and building stewardship as a spiritual practice." How might such work unfold and develop? First of all, think in the long term. To discover and build stewardship as a spiritual practice is a five-year piece of work. You won't get this done by next Tuesday, or in three months, or even within a year. Part of the reason is that, in an established congregation, people have learned other ways to think about and approach stewardship. Often, for example, our approach to stewardship is institutional and budget-driven. When that is the case, the mindset is: "How much money do we need to keep the church going next year?" Often a figure has been determined in the budget process. The budget committee chair says to the stewardship chair: "You'll need to raise 7 percent more than last year, because health insurance premiums have gone up a good bit, and we are going to need to do something about the roof on the C.E. building." So the stewardship committee makes its theme "The 7 Percent Solution," and it promotes the idea that all members give 7 percent more than they did last year. After "Stewardship Sunday" in November, about half the pledges are in. Optimistic projections indicate that the drive will come up about $50,000 short, and by January that is where things stand. The stewardship and budget chairs call a special meeting, and together they make the same appeal they did two years ago: those who have already pledged should "go the second mile" and up their pledge. This scenario is pretty common, and it is not at

ture: A Strategic and Spiritual Approach (Herndon, VA: Alban Institute, 1996); Lovett Weems, Taking the Next Step: Leading Lasting Change in the Church (Nashville: Abingdon, 2003), esp. chs. 3-5; see also Carl S. Dudley and Nancy T. Ammerman, Congregations in Transition: A Guide for Analyzing, Assessing, and Adapting in Changing Congregations (San Francisco: Jossey-Bass, 2002). The Alban Institute (www.alban.org) also offers a number of other resources and guides for congregational planning.

all life-giving! It is not stewardship as a spiritual practice, but stewardship that is budget-driven and focuses on the institutional aspect alone.

A pastoral leader might begin by asking members of the governing board and stewardship committee to read and discuss a book or article that takes a different approach, one more in keeping with stewardship as a spiritual practice.[2] The leader could also suggest Scripture passages such as Matthew 25:14-30 (the parable of the talents) or Luke 12:13-21 (the parable of the rich fool). At this point leaders are doing two things: first, *framing the challenge* and doing so in fresh ways (for example, "Maybe it's not just a matter of meeting the budget, maybe it's related to our purpose, 'Growing people of faith'"); second, leaders are *enriching the soil* with new information, with fresh perspectives, and by changing the conversation.

Gradually, leaders can extend some of this discussion to other groups and to the congregation as a whole, perhaps through sermons, selected reprints in the newsletter, or information and suggestions on the website. In addition, leaders will *turn up the heat* by thoughtfully indicating some ways that current practice isn't working. For example, information might be provided to the congregation that indicates that giving levels have hit a plateau, or that the congregation as a whole is currently giving at a 1.5 percent level in relation to personal income (common among mainline churches), or by describing how the "second mile" pattern is really counterproductive in the long run. At this point, the governing board might be asked to appoint a group that will begin to discuss options for a new way of doing things, one that will advance stewardship as a spiritual practice. All of the moves that are italicized above are forms of *ripening the challenge,* which means making people aware of the work and preparing the congregational soil. This takes time — perhaps a year or even two.

In time, the task force on stewardship as a spiritual practice comes up with a proposal for the governing board, one that will shape how stewardship is done next fall. The task force sets aside the goal of "meeting the budget"; rather, the new goal is "growing a congregation of generous people" who experience a powerful connection between their faith/spirituality and their stewardship. The task force plans a different kind of steward-

2. For possible discussion material, see Anthony B. Robinson, *Transforming Congregational Culture* (Grand Rapids: Eerdmans, 2003), ch. 10; see also Michael Durrell, *Creating Congregations of Generous People* (Herndon, VA: Alban Institute, 1999).

ship program for the coming autumn: it will pair up members of the congregation, whether singles or couples or families, and will provide a resource for discussing "The Role of Money in Our Lives and Faith." Leaders ask people to meet with their pair partner(s) during the two-week stewardship time to work through the discussion guide and then to complete their pledge. The discussion guide for pair meetings invites people to discuss questions such as "How have you experienced God's presence in the life of our church during this past year?" "What is an early memory of money in your life?" "How do you think about the relationship between money and faith in your life?" "Do you find that your giving to God through the church is meaningful? Why or why not?"

Meanwhile, the new stewardship team has put before the congregation a challenge goal, one that they themselves have each accepted: "I/we are committed to work toward giving 5 percent of my/our personal annual income to God's work through our church and its mission and ministry. I believe that in doing so I will grow in the practice of generosity and experience stewardship as integral to my spiritual life and growth." (Note how this links back to congregational purpose.) In the first year of such a new venture and approach, and also during the second and third year, leaders will need to be prepared to *manage distress.* Some church members will respond enthusiastically, others with caution, and still others with strong resistance. Be prepared for the varied responses and for the resistance. Distress can be managed in a number of ways. It is important to keep purpose and vision before the congregation and to remind them of how this new approach to stewardship relates to both. If the resistance level is too high, slow the pace of the work, but don't give up.

Where success happens, share it, celebrate it, and build on it. Remember that you are changing the culture of a congregation and that takes time, resilience, and persistence. Leaders will need to *maintain disciplined attention* to the key adaptive work and be alert to inevitable work avoidance on the part of some. An example of work avoidance might be: "We're spending way too much time and energy on money. Doing good work in the community is what's important!"[3] As congrega-

---

3. For more on these leadership strategies, see Robinson, *Transforming Congregational Culture,* ch. 13; see also Robinson, *Leadership for Vital Congregations* (Cleveland: Pilgrim Press, 2006), and Ron Heifetz and Marty Linsky, *Leadership on the Line* (Cambridge, MA: Harvard Business School Press, 2002).

tional leaders maintain disciplined attention and stay with this work of moving from budget-driven, institution-minded stewardship to stewardship as a spiritual practice and growing congregations of generous people, the congregation will turn a corner in three to five years. People will have experienced learning and change; they will have grown in their faith and in their practice of faith. Furthermore, the practice of generosity and stewardship as spiritual practice will have become part of the new culture of the congregation.

Deepening Adult Spiritual Formation

Again, as in the matter of stewardship, we are not working with a *tabula rasa,* a blank slate. Most congregations have something in place, and they have notions about the right way to do things, usually inherited from the Christendom era. That era taught us a couple of things that are no longer true or helpful. First among them was that most everyone was sort of a Christian by virtue of growing up in North America; second, that we could count on the culture (public schools, families, holiday practices, and auxiliary groups such as Boy Scouts, lodges, and service clubs) to do Christian formation for us, for the church. We did not really have to work at Christian formation because it pretty much happened naturally in American Christendom. While it varies in different regions of North America, this is mostly gone: congregations that depend on the culture to do Christian formation for them have been running into trouble for thirty years or more. Moreover, the church formed by Christendom tended to see children as the primary focus for Christian education, while adults went to worship. Today both children and adults need both spiritual formation and worship if faith is to flourish and grow (purpose again).

Once again, the starting point is framing the challenge. It might be framed in the following way: How can we help adults who have never before been Christians discover and grow in Christian faith and life? And how can our church help those who have long been Christians deepen their faith and find in it new meaning and power? Another way to put it might be: What is our process for helping people become disciples of Jesus? Answers to these challenges will not only come in the church's teaching ministry but in worship, fellowship, and in our experiences of practicing faith and discipleship in outreach and evangelism.

Indeed, it is possible that the church's purpose and life may be wholly focused on its process for spiritual growth or for making disciples, an option to which I shall return shortly.

But here we focus on a particular part of the church's life, the teaching ministry and its role in adult Christian formation. Leaders begin by *framing* and *ripening* the challenge. Again, leaders can use books, articles, speakers, and videotapes to help key people see things in fresh ways, to identify paradigms of the past that are no longer helpful, and to begin to imagine new possibilities. Ripening the work proceeds by once again *enriching the soil* with reading, discussion, sermons, and Scripture study. All of this moves toward the end of helping growing numbers of people become aware of the adaptive challenge of deepening their adult spiritual formation. Leaders may consider selective ways to *turn up the heat.* Perhaps leaders will draw a verbal portrait of a new young adult in the church who has no church or spiritual background but is eager and hungry. That's a different kind of person than Christendom prepared us for. Or leaders might relate a few stories of older adults whose children are not involved in church but who do participate in practices of spiritual deepening through meditation or yoga. Why, leaders might wonder, have these adults turned elsewhere for spiritual growth?

Next, one of the groups in the congregation, perhaps a task group or team, or the church staff, or an existing education board or committee, will explore options for deepening adult Christian formation. They might explore several options, and then, with time and plenty of preparation, might try them. One strategy is to develop a small-group ministry that is clearly focused on spirituality and spiritual growth. There are many resources available for such groups and programs. Leadership training is the key. It is also important to set the expectations and establish guidelines that will make the groups safe and keep them focused on their primary purpose, that is, spiritual deepening.

A more ambitious strategy, but one that I have seen work, is to move from the one-hour-on-Sunday model to a two-hour model and expectation. The one-hour model of Christendom was worship for adults, Sunday school for children — both activities occurring simultaneously, and everything done in an hour.[4] In contrast, the two-hour approach

---

4. For more on the downsides of the "one-hour-on-Sunday" model, see *Transforming Congregational Culture*, chs. 4-5.

would mean an hour of teaching ministry, followed by an hour of worship; both children and adults would participate in both. This does ask more of people, and not everyone will buy into it — at least not right away. But stay on purpose, keep purpose and vision before the people, and call attention to how a shift to a two-hour experience (actually, it will probably be closer to two and a half or three hours) not only asks more but it gives more in return and keeps the church "on purpose."

Specifically, what might this look like? I'll just give one illustration, but there are a variety of possibilities. During the first hour children would participate in a lectionary-based Sunday school program, while adults would take part in a *lectio divina* practice of Scripture study also based on the lectionary text(s); those texts would also be the basis of the worship service in the second hour. One asset of the *lectio divina* practice and format is that leaders do not need to be Bible scholars or experts. They need to be able to gently "mind the process" and keep the group on task, which is listening to Scripture, to God, to themselves, and to others. Then, in the second hour, all congregation members worship together. Again, there will be distress and resistance to intergenerational worship, and moving toward such a change will need to be very well prepared and deliberate. But it has been my experience that, with time, patience, and positive reinforcement, children learn the rhythms of worship, and their parents and grandparents can learn to live with — and worship with — their children. If the worship leaders use the lectionary, it becomes a way to link the teaching and worship ministry.

Once again, this will take time: it is another five-year piece of work to frame the work, prepare the soil, ready the planting of the new seed, nurture it, keep the weeds and brambles at bay, continue to water and fertilize the plants, and experience the harvest. Leaders will need to be ready to manage distress and deal with resistance. They will have to maintain disciplined attention, to frame and reframe the work, and to be resilient, adaptive, and persistent. And they will have to be ready to give out a lot of positive reinforcement! In this brief case study I am not in any way attempting to exhaustively work through "deepening adult spiritual formation," only to illustrate it. I have tried to emphasize that doing this work requires thinking sequentially, pacing the work so that people are challenged but not too much, and dealing with predictable distress, resistance, and push-backs. Furthermore, I have tried to emphasize that such work takes time, patience, and persistence. As we turn to other adaptive challenges in the next two chapters, all of these points remain salient.

Christian Formation: Program or Process?

What I have described above is a new "program" for Christian formation. But it may be that the entire concept of programs and program churches are a holdover from the era of establishment, or Christendom. A more radical approach is to put the emphasis less on a program and more on a process, one of Christian growth and formation that guides and permeates all aspects of the congregation's life.

For Rick Warren, who urges that we put the emphasis on growing people through a process rather than creating programs, that process is fourfold and can be captured in the image of a baseball diamond. Getting to first is moving from interest to membership; taking second base means growing to mature faith; reaching third base is claiming one's ministry; and arriving at home plate is a person's life purpose or mission.[5] Another church may describe its process for spiritual growth in terms of spaces, or rooms: a person moves from the foyer to the living room to the kitchen of the church and Christian life. Still others speak of a threefold process of connection, growing, and serving.

While such sequences and metaphors for the process can become overdone and formulaic, they do not need to turn into gimmicks; they are ways of acknowledging that Christian life and growth has steps, stages, or seasons. Part of every learning experience consists of breaking the subject down into elements, steps, or parts. This is one of the processes that makes Alcoholics Anonymous and other twelve-step programs effective. Participants have something to hang their hats on, so to speak. They can say, "I'm working on Step Four" or "I'm back at Step One." The point is not to move through the steps as fast as possible, but to be aware of the different tasks involved in recovery and growth.

The authors of various treatments of discipleship, whether Rick Warren in *The Purpose Driven Church* or Jeffrey Jones in *Traveling Together*, lay out some pattern for growth and development. Classical

---

5. Rick Warren, *The Purpose Driven Church* (Grand Rapids: Zondervan, 1995), pp. 309ff.

Christian thought also offers such a pattern and may suggest a starting place for congregations and leaders who want to help their participants have a sense of the sequence of spiritual formation. In classical theology, the three major elements of the Christian life are justification, sanctification, and vocation. In one sense, they are sequential, each following the other; in another sense, they are more like spirals that weave in and out of each other. *Justification* means God's action on our behalf to restore us to a relationship with God, with self, and with others. It is Christ who, though he did not know sin, was made sin for our sakes. It entails our surrender, our coming to God and God's coming to us, our receiving grace, and our knowing mercy and a peace that the world cannot give. It is the grace of a loving God that eluded Luther for so long; it is John Wesley's "heart strangely warmed." It is John Newton's "Amazing Grace": "I once was lost but now am found, was blind but now I see." Some faith communities use the word "conversion," while others use "transformation." In either case it is a turning, a dying to the self-centered and fearful self and being raised to a new life centered in God, our true self, and our neighbor. It happens once and it happens many times.

Sanctification means being made holy, being set apart by and for God. Sanctification is God's work and is our work — or better, it is God's continuing work in us. Grace, though free, is not cheap: it requires a response. From the basic and elemental experience of having a broken bone reset in justification, we experience sanctification as a growing in health and strength, as we exercise our formerly fractured part in the practice of faith. Sanctification means growing up in Christ, growing to spiritual maturity. If justification is setting a broken life for healing, and sanctification is growing and strengthening that life, *vocation* is what that life is called to and used for by God. From the Latin verb *vocare* ("to call"), vocation means that we hear or discern what God wants, and how God wants us to give and use our life for God's glory and for mending God's creation. Vocation is more than a particular job, though the jobs we have may be one way we express and live out our vocation. Or our job may be the way we put food on the table and provide for a family, and our vocation is what we do when we sit down late in the evening to write or compose music, or when we parent and raise children, or when we serve the poor.

My aim here is not to fully discuss these three major movements of the Christian life; it is only to suggest that congregations who take adult formation seriously will find ways to talk about steps, stages, seasons, and sequences in the Christian life. Moreover, they may begin to think less in terms of their church *program,* and more in terms of their formation or spiritual growth *process.* Christian formation is a lifelong process. By differentiating and sequencing, we do not overcome the mystery of spiritual formation, but we can more fully and readily embrace it.

For Reflection and Discussion

- How would you describe the way your congregation currently goes about spiritual or Christian formation?
- How do you respond to shifting the emphasis from our Christian education "program" to our formation/spiritual growth "process"?

Let's Get (Less) Organized!

You may think of the subject of church organization as the dullest of the dull. Think again. It's not only important, it's even dangerous. Actually, the whole organization subject is a minefield upon which the wise set foot only with great caution. This is partly true because there are people in many congregations who cling to their church bylaws with considerably more ardor than they do to Holy Scripture! Simultaneously, at the other extreme, "restructuring" beckons to others like the Holy Grail, promising new life. But as in the quest for the Grail, restructuring can kill you! Given these dangers, why mess with it? Why not leave well enough alone, work with the existing structures, or work around them?

The most important answer is that the organizational structures of most long-established congregations were created for the era of American Christendom and modernity. They worked pretty well in their time, but we don't live there anymore. Here's another way to put that: the organizational structures of many congregations are designed for maintenance, not mission. That is, they are designed to maintain the local church of the Christendom era but not to engage the culture as a mission outpost of God's new creation.

This basic point can be elaborated in a couple ways. Underlying the Christendom-era structures of church life are two notions: (1) the best way to involve people in Christian life and church participation is to get them serving on a board or committee of the church; and (2) the job of laity is to manage the church. If your church assumes that the best way to involve people in Christian life and the church is to get them on a board or committee, there's a good chance that your congregation will have a lot of boards and committees to accommodate them. The result is often structures that are either Byzantine in complexity or Catch-22-like in absurdity. The second unhelpful assumption is that the really important job of lay Christians is to manage the church, its buildings, finances, property, and personnel. This effectively takes the team off the playing field and gives it the task of managing the clubhouse. Instead of inviting people to *do* ministry, current systems invite them to *manage* the ministry. You put these two assumptions together and let the whole thing settle for some decades, and the result would make for a good Monty Python skit.

For example, here is the picture of one congregation whose pastor consulted with me not long ago. That congregation's organizational structure provides for 92 positions to be filled by nomination and election. The congregation has 110 members, and the pastor estimates that, of that number, 48 are able-bodied, participating adults. The other 62 are elderly people who may get out of the house for Sunday morning worship but little else; people who have moved away but have maintained their membership; confirmed teens or college students who are away at school; and military personnel, also absent because they are in service. This basic scenario is repeated often these days: more slots — many more — than there are people. Even if everyone agrees to wear two or three hats (this would be the Monty Python material), it's still a stretch.

One imagines a puzzled denominational official saying to a lay member:

"But I thought you were the chairperson of the council. I wanted to meet with the head of the finance committee."

"This year I head finance, too," is the person's reply. "But don't worry — it's just temporary."

"Great! How long have you held down both positions?" asks the official.

"Fourteen years."

"Do you expect the Sunday school superintendent can make it to the meeting?"

"You're looking at her!" answers the council chair and finance committee head.

The response to such a mismatch between structure and reality is often to insist that reality must change. So people in such situations, the land of many hats, will say, "What we need here are more members." The structure and organizational manifest require more people to fill the slots; but we do not have more people; therefore, we must grow in numbers. Besides the oddity of allowing the structure to dictate the mission, this doesn't work anyway. Few people are attracted by an appeal that takes the form of "Join our church so we can fill up our boards and committees!"

Larger congregations face pretty much the same thing. Another church of 900 members has enough people, in theory, to fill its 176 positions; but it still has vacancies. "People are too busy," laments one such pastor. "Every two-parent family in my congregation has two jobs that are more than full-time. When you add in schlepping the kids here and there and an occasional weekend away, serving on a board that meets monthly and has one or two subcommittee assignments — well, forget it!" While people in smaller congregations assume that larger congregations don't have these problems and believe that the answer is more members, it rarely seems to work out that way. Yet the problem may not be, as the above pastor assumes, that "people are too busy."

While people *are* busy (it is practically un-American not to be), people will find the time for what matters to them and for what energizes them. I suspect that, beyond busy-ness, too often the jobs we ask people to do are not life-giving precisely because they are about maintaining structures and systems for an era that ended thirty or more years ago. They are not structures that are doing truly engaging and important work in our new time. It is a little like maintaining an antiquated association or club that was very important to our grandparents. We may do it as a yearly task out of a mixture of sentimentality and devotion, but it is not where we live. This takes us back to purpose and to structures that are derived from a clear, compelling, and core purpose. Instead of having the proverbial tail (the structure) wag the dog (the purpose/mission), we must meet the adaptive challenge of making the dog wag the tail again.

Before we take up the question of what that might look like, allow me to make two further observations about the current organization and structure of many churches. I have mentioned above that in the Christendom era we tended to imagine that the job of dedicated lay Christians was to maintain and manage the church facility, finances, and ministry. "Ministry" in the Christendom era was done by clergy, staff, and maybe a few lay leaders: it meant providing religious services (baptism, funerals, counseling, hospital visitation, prayer and worship, community presence and participation) and programs (confirmation, youth groups, social groups) for the members of the congregation. In our new time we may need to rethink this assumption that the "ministry is done," by and large, by ordained ministers and paid staff.

What if the ministry is not something done largely or entirely by the ordained clergy or the church staff? What if it belongs to and is done by the people, the members of the church? Such is the implication of the apostle Paul's words that the task of leaders (such as Paul himself) is to "equip the saints for ministry" in the world. Imagine a church where the ministry is not done entirely — or even mainly — by the ordained minister(s) but by the baptized, the people of God. That ministry is not primarily managing the church; it is what lay Christians do in their own vocations and workplaces, in their relationships with others, in their participation as citizens, and in their daily lives. Could it be that the real job of dedicated Christians is not to manage the work of the ordained or the operational administration of the church facility, but to represent Christ to the world? I suspect that many would affirm this in theory, yet our church structures tend not to support the theory. Getting many folks involved in operating and maintaining the church worked reasonably well in the Christendom era. But it may be a serious misstep in a time when the mission field has moved: no longer overseas or at the borders of nation or empire, but all around us.

With the mission field all around us, ministry properly belongs to the people, the laity. The job of the ordained is to equip the people for their ministry in the world. There is a corollary to this: I find that thriving and vital congregations not only tend to give the ministry back to the people, but the people of the congregation entrust the leadership of the church to those who have been called or elected for that task. When the current arrangement dysfunctions, you will have a large number of laypeople, even the whole congregation in churches with smaller memberships, trying to run or lead the church; and you will have very few people doing ministry in and for the world. In our new time we need to work toward a church where the leaders entrust the ministry to the congregation, and where the congregation entrusts leadership to those called and elected to those tasks.

Not only do our current structures of church life and their underlying assumptions reflect the era of American Christendom; they have also been formed by the values and assumptions of modernity. Modernity, with its emphasis on the rational and the functional, imagined the church as a smooth-running machine or factory: you get all the parts in place, keep the thing well oiled and operating smoothly, and you have a successful church. The parts in this case tended to be a prescribed organizational structure: council, trustees, deacons, men's department, women's department, children and youth, missions, and so on. Smaller congregations assumed that this was how church is supposed to look; so they took on — or tried to take on — the organizational structures and goal-directed ethos of their bigger cousins and neighbors. The unspoken assumption in many smaller congregations, as I have observed before, is: "Someday we will grow up and become a real church." That means, someday we will have enough people to fill all the positions and programs that real churches have.

I recently worked with a new church start that was off to a great beginning. Some of the members who had belonged to other congregations before coming to the new one assumed that getting such a structure in place was imperative and would mean that the new church was really a church. I suggested that, rather than borrowing the organizational model from another time, they ask, "What structure do we need to further our missional purpose?"

"Give yourselves permission," I suggested, "not to assume that structures you have known elsewhere are normative for all times and places or necessarily for you." They have developed a more streamlined and flexible organizational structure that seems to be serving them well.

Operating from the assumptions of modernity, you may end up with a very effective organization, but is it a church? Church, more or less by definition, is Christ-led and Spirit-empowered. And yet our image of the successful church of the modern era was like most things modern: the smoothly functioning machine. The result, of course, was church machines, not spiritual communities. A good bit of our devotion to organizational structures owes more to modernity than to Christian conviction. The reason that many restructuring efforts, whether at the congregational or denominational level, run aground is that they are still driven by modernist assumptions: they say, for example, "We have duplication here," or "We have inefficiencies there," or "We can consolidate these functions over there." Such restructuring efforts are not guided by purpose or mission. The key is to have a powerful, compelling sense of purpose/mission; when we have that in place, the organizational structures will follow and get worked out. When we do not have that in place, or when our purpose statements are lofty but unreal rhetoric, we will spend countless hours rearranging the sinking ship's deck chairs as energy drains away.

Let's pull these observations together in summary form as follows:

- The structures of most long-established mainline congregations were designed for the era of American Christendom.
- The Christendom era assigned "ministry" to the minister(s), the ordained, and the credentialed; it assigned the maintenance and administration of the church to the laity.
- The overlay of modernity put an emphasis on the church as a smoothly functioning machine of many parts.
- The adaptive challenge now is to ask: "Given why we are here, given our purpose/mission — that is, what we're trying to accomplish — how do we best organize ourselves?

Questions for Reflection and Discussion
- Which parts of the introduction to this chapter ring true for you and your church? Do some parts not ring true?
- What concerns you most about the subject of restructuring or redesigning how your church operates?

A Systems Approach to Church Life and Organization

My hunch is that making progress on this adaptive challenge, structuring and organizing the church's life for our new time, will entail some experimentation with this and that to see what might work. With good humor, grace, and God's help, you'll work out a way of doing things that probably won't be perfect but will be an improvement. Moreover, as I argued in the preceding section of this conversation, the real issue or question is purpose. If purpose is in place and is powerful, the organization will get sorted out. If purpose is not in place, if we don't know why we're here or what we're trying to accomplish, we can work on structure and organization until the cows come home and it won't amount to much. With that in mind, let me suggest a different approach to organization, one that is driven by purpose and one that departs from modernist values and assumptions. Call it a "systems approach" to church life.

If modernity tended to think of the church as a machine or factory, a postmodern alternative would be to think of the church as a living system — for example, a garden, a stream, or a forest. In a living system the parts are connected and interdependent. For the parts to thrive, the whole must thrive; conversely, for the whole to be vital, each of the parts must also be vital. A stream requires water flowing in, a rich streambed that supports fish and smaller life forms, a stream bottom and banks that are stable, and then a way for the water to flow out. One might think of that as an analogy for the living system of the church. There is the in-flow side, which might be thought of as a congregation's inviting, welcoming, and hospitality ministry, and also as the in-flow of new life experience among present participants. The second part of the system is everything in a congregation's life that grows people's faith, or through which the Holy Spirit works to grow people of faith: worship, education or teaching ministry, and perhaps some form of small-group experience. The third part of such a purpose-based system would be equipping and sending people out into the world to be instruments of God's grace and presence. Like the stream, water flows in; the water then both supports life and is enriched and changed; then the water flows on.

In a systems approach to church life, the system has three basic parts: inviting and welcoming, growing or transforming, equipping and sending. One pastor, whose congregation thinks of its purpose as "being and making disciples," said that her congregation sums up its life as "bringing 'em in," "growing 'em up," and "sending 'em out." In a real sense, this describes the weekly rhythm of the church. We are called and gathered, we are led into God's transforming presence, and then we scatter into the world as God's people. Week by week we are gathered, touched, and taught, and then we are sent out.

In such a systems approach, all three parts of the system are interdependent. You cannot put all your eggs into one basket, that is, emphasize one of the parts at the expense of the others. And yet such malignancy is common in the more mechanistic or departmental approach to church structures that was shaped by modernity. Support for the music program means cutting back on social justice work; or putting more emphasis on evangelism means that we will have to cut back on the youth program. In such structures you tend to have competition, not interdependence. Rather than parts of a whole system, you typically end up with programmatic silos, each one independent (or imagining that it is) and each doing its own thing. In one church, some will strive to build the music program, while in another it is all about "missions." If we use the human body as an analogy to the body of Christ, we don't call it success when one part grows excessively and without check — we call it cancer!

Whether this simple systems approach becomes a blueprint for an organizational structure or not, it suggests several important points. First, the *structure* is driven by the *purpose*. A stream or a forest that is healthy develops a structure that naturally supports its purpose, whether it is to grow strong trees within a forest ecosystem or to move clean water and sustain life all along the way. If the purpose is clear and compelling, the structure will follow. Second, the parts of a system are interrelated and mutually dependent. No stream system would do very well if the banks said, "It's all about the banks of the stream — to heck with the fish and the water!"

A congregation might organize itself along the lines of the three component parts of this simple system. There could be the inviting ministry, which might include invitational evangelism, public relations, and hospitality. But it's not just about welcoming new people; it's also about welcoming the flow of new life experience among the people already there. Then there could be the transforming and forming ministry: this would include worship and teaching, or formational groups. The third component would be the sending ministry of gifts discernment, equipping, service, and ministry teams. These three — inviting, transforming, and sending — could become the core ministries or structures. Still, my point here is not so much to commend this as an organizational structure as to suggest that the organization of a congregation's life be thought of as a living system. The nature of the system is derived from the purpose of the church.

For Reflection and Discussion

- How do you respond to the "systems approach" described in this section? What excites you about it? What concerns do you have?

- Do you feel that your own congregation has a clear and compelling purpose or mission? Does the organizational life of your congregation support that purpose?

Getting Less Organized — Further Thoughts

In the concluding portion of this conversation I will present an organizational format that I have worked on with several congregations. Again, my intention is not to say, "Here's the way to do it," but, "Here's one way I've done it. Maybe this will give you something to build on, to modify, and to experiment with in your own situation." Remember that the key first step is reasonable clarity about a compelling purpose and mission. Without that, restructuring efforts in long-established congregations tend to proceed from the given structure, and then determine how we can accommodate all the interests represented in that structure — while streamlining just a little.

Let's start with this purpose or mission statement: "Growing people of faith who participate in God's work in the world." Then there are three basic components to this governance system: a governing board, core ministry teams, and flexible ministry teams.

The Governing Board

It is pretty standard for churches to have some entity that has the responsibility of a governing board or body. It may be the session, the consistory, the council, or the vestry. Some of these may actually function as governing bodies, but most such bodies content themselves with information exchange. Various program boards or committees whose heads are represented on the governing group make monthly reports. Often the governing group is quite large: twenty-five to thirty-five people or positions. Congregations do need a governing and leadership group, but that group should actually govern and lead and not merely hear reports from individuals representing other boards and committees. Such a body should not exceed fifteen members, and it need not be composed of the chairs of all other boards and committees. By all means, governing groups should have ways to get input from those committees; but composing your governing body from the chairs of all other groups in the church makes individual board members think of their jobs mainly as representing their group or constituency and its interests. You want people on the governing board who are thinking in terms of the whole and the parts of the church in relationship, not just focusing on their particular part.

Beyond the questions of size and makeup of the governing board, what are its tasks? To put it in a nutshell, a governing board governs: it does not manage or micro-manage day-to-day operations. Its number-one task is to discern the purpose for which God has called the congregation into being, and then to orchestrate the process that arrives at the vision or strategic plan for the next three, five, or ten years. With the help of the pastoral staff, the governing board must keep purpose and vision before the congregation. This is its leadership function. Second, a governing board develops necessary church policies; third, it ensures that administrative systems and functions are in place and are being accomplished. Typically, these systems include personnel management (or human resources) and financial and facilities management. The point is not for a governing board to *do* the day-to-day operational management, but to make sure that it gets done.

Core Ministry Teams

With purpose in place, every congregation will have several core ministries that it understands as essential to fulfilling its purpose. These might be *inviting, transforming,* and *sending.* One way to identify core ministries is to ask the "vital few" question. That is, what are the vital few things that our church must do and do well to be faithful to the purpose for which God has called us? What is essential? If our purpose is "to grow people of faith who participate in God's work in the world," the vital few might include inviting/hospitality, worship and formation (teaching and small groups), and equipping and sending ministries. These are the key elements of what you do as a church that must, in the judgment of the governing board or congregation, be reliably in place. There would be a core ministry team charged with managing each ministry area. Note the word "management" here: it is not the task of persons serving on a core ministry team to reinvent the wheel (or the ministry) with each new group that joins the body. The program or ministry is a given, established in relationship to the purpose, and it is the job of the core ministry team to manage this program effectively.

In the modern era and model, such groups were often highly routinized. For example, they would meet monthly, no more and no less, on a scheduled night each month. Each group would consist of a uniform number of members. Such prescriptions may not always be helpful. For example, one core ministry of the church is probably going to be worship. Many congregations have a worship board or committee that meets once a month. Such a format is not usually very helpful in worship planning, because worship occurs weekly, if not more often. Instead of a worship board or worship committee, many congregations seem to do better with a worship planning team that meets weekly. It may be made up mostly of church staff, or it may be made up of a mix of staff and laypeople. The point is that the frequency of meetings, the nature of the meetings, and the composition of the group may vary depending on the group's ministry and work.

Flexible Ministry Teams

Unlike the core teams that manage the vital few ministries of the congregation, the flexible teams may come and go in response to members' sense of calling, as well as to available time and interest. For the most part, these ministry teams will be ways that laypeople do their ministry in the world. So there may be a "Habitat for Humanity" team, a team that prepares and serves meals at a homeless shelter, a team that does tutoring for immigrants, a team that lobbies at the state legislature, and a group of people working in healthcare who get together to support one another in that vocation. Teams arise in response to two or more members' passion and sense of calling to do some form of ministry that is consistent with the church's purpose, vision, and values. At the church I most recently served, we moved to this format during my ministry. When I concluded my ministry at that congregation, there were 42 such ministry teams, and today there are 64. A congregation will need to put a simple process in place for authorizing a team. Moreover, it is crucial to be clear on the following point: the *responsibility for the success of a ministry team rests with the ministry team.* In other words, members of the church staff may (or may not) provide advice and support, but they are not responsible for the team; the team leader(s) and members are.

Flexible ministry teams can be supported in two ways. First, there may be a person (paid or unpaid) who is responsible for ministry teams and will coordinate information flow and communication and will develop gifts-discernment events and programs for people to use to identify their gifts for ministry and to connect with a team. The other important responsibility for this staff person will be to provide training events for potential and actual ministry team leaders. These leaders are the key people: for such a system to work, leaders must be trained, equipped, and supported. This might happen through a monthly or quarterly gathering of all ministry team leaders for consultation and support, or it may be more informal.

Church Staff

In reality, there is a fourth part to this system, and it is a crucial part: your church staff. During the Christendom era, churches tended to be very high on volunteer involvement and relied on volunteers for all sorts of things around the church, from mowing the lawn to fixing the plumbing to keeping the books. Today churches tend to rely less on volunteers and more on people who are employed or contracted to do that work. This is partly because, as consultant George Barna observes, "Time is the new currency." People have limited time. In some congregations they have more money to hire someone to keep the books than they have time to do it themselves. I see nothing wrong with this, and potentially there is a great deal that is right with it: the work that is hired out will probably be done in a more professional and timely fashion.

If there are people who feel called by God to maintain the church grounds and they really do the job, that's great. But I'm not so sure it's a great idea to have volunteers or church members keeping the books, fixing the roof, or doing the painting. As has often been observed, it's pretty hard to fire a volunteer. So, even if the volunteer is not doing a good job, or even if he or she is chronically late in meeting deadlines or commitments, you're stuck with that person. Church members voice their opposition to hiring the work out by saying, "We can't afford it."

Actually, that is usually a choice, and often not a wise one. Most mainline Protestant individuals or families support their churches at a relatively low financial level (1.5 to 2 percent of annual income is average). Get the giving where it ought to be — say, 5 percent — and you'll be able to employ people to do the necessary work.

For Reflection and Discussion
- What do you find exciting about this church structure (governing board, core ministries, flexible ministry teams)? What concerns do you have?
- What would you say are the "vital few" for your church?

Right-Sizing or Restructuring as an Adaptive Challenge

Like "Stewardship as a Spiritual Practice" and "Deepening Adult Christian Formation," "Let's Get (Less) Organized" constitutes an adaptive challenge. Here are several suggestions for leading this adaptive work, using terms from Ron Heifetz's book *Leadership without Easy Answers*.[1]

Part of the job of leaders is to *name* and *frame* the work. You could describe it as "developing a structure to support our purpose/mission" or "evolving our structure to a new time." Naming and framing the work is part of *ripening the adaptive work,* that is, making the congregation aware of the challenge and putting it on the agenda. These two steps, naming and ripening, will probably take two years — maybe more. Soon after arriving at one of my congregations, I proposed a staff position for a coordinator of shared ministry. It went nowhere. Twelve years later, however, after a whole lot of naming and ripening and building, the position came into being. It is now firmly a part of that church's life.

As the work begins to get the congregation's attention, leaders will need to *anticipate and manage distress.* Managing distress can mean either turning up the heat or lowering it. In order for people to learn and change, they usually need to be feeling some level of distress, some heat. However, if they feel too much distress, or they feel it's too hot, they will shut down. Here are a couple of examples of what I mean by "turning

---

1. Ronald Heifetz, *Leadership without Easy Answers* (Cambridge, MA: Harvard Belknap Press, 1993).

up the heat." The pastor of the church mentioned at the beginning of this conversation might write an article for the congregation's newsletter noting that the current governing structure has 92 positions but the congregation has only 48 available persons. Perhaps that same pastor, or a group of lay leaders, could write a kind of Monty Python skit about that absurdity for the annual talent night. Or similar things might be done, for example, in the congregation where a survey indicated that, among the 1,100 members, 42 people were interested in serving in the 140 board or committee positions, but over 700 individuals were interested in being involved in ministry teams. Such information turns up the heat for doing adaptive work.

Lowering the heat might sound like this: "Now, don't get alarmed. We understand that good financial management is important and we will not compromise on that." Or you can say, "What we're proposing is a two-year experiment with a new kind of church council. We will have some checkpoints along the way and an evaluation after twenty-one months. Your input will be important to us." Or you can say, "A study of our congregation's 180-year history indicates that we have had major reorganizations at least seven times in the past. This is nothing new."

Managing distress or anxiety may also mean providing reading material, speakers, and stories from other congregations that have dealt with similar challenges, as well as congregations that have made positive changes. Leaders will need to *take resistance seriously* by listening for valid concerns and criticism, by avoiding being defensive, and by staying connected to the people who are resisting. Taking resistance seriously does not mean backing down. But it does mean that, while you maintain your principles, you need to stay connected to people. Leaders will also need to plan successes along the way and *celebrate those successes.* A study is completed, celebrate it! A presentation is planned and given, celebrate it. Confronting adaptive challenges is tough work. To make progress, you need to value small steps and celebrate successes.

Above all, leaders will need to *keep the work before* the people and *externalize the work,* by which I mean this: if you are the minister or a key lay leader in this initiative, try to avoid letting the work become personalized or internalized. It's not about you! Move it away from you (i.e., externalize it) by continually describing it as an important challenge facing the church. Focus on the work, not on personalities.

The entire sequence from beginning to end — and the end means having a new and more effective structure in place as a firm part of the congregation's culture — is at least a five-year piece of work. A final note: there is no perfect structure this side of the kingdom of God. There are only structures that are better or worse. But moving away from those paradigms of getting everyone on a board or committee and having most laypeople involved in church management is worthwhile, important work. Don't give up!

The Church and the Public Square

The subject of this conversation constitutes another key adaptive challenge facing congregations and their leaders in our new time. What is the role of the church in the public life of America? Once, during the era of American Christendom and the dominance of the Protestant mainline denominations, answers to this question were clear. Our job was to be the conscience of the community, the instrument of aid for the less fortunate, and the center of family and community life. We no longer enjoy such clarity, but that doesn't mean that congregations and their leaders can simply roll over on the matter of the church's public involvement or role. This really is a most important conversation to have.

While a conversation about the public role of congregations and their leaders might not seem to fit with the other conversations here, in another sense it is of a piece with all that has gone before in this book. In particular, it is similar to "Stewardship as a Spiritual Practice" and "Deepening Adult Spiritual Formation" in Conversation 6, as well as "Let's Get (Less) Organized" in Conversation 7. Each of those topics identifies and engages a crucial challenge faced by congregations in our new time. This conversation about the role of the church in public life in our society is like those: here we encounter an adaptive challenge facing the church. Unlike the first three, which are focused more on the internal life and ministry of the church and the personal faith of its members, this one is more external, or public.

As an adaptive challenge, engaging the role of congregations in the public square will require learning and change. A technical solution that uses existing techniques and is carried out by experts and authorities is not enough. Congregations and their leaders need to rethink, reframe, and embody their public role and witness in fresh ways as they respond to our post-Christendom, postmodern time. When this work is reduced to a "technical problem," it tends to become the search for new ethical and spiritual "giants." We ask where the Niebuhrs, the Tillichs, the Harry Emerson Fosdicks, and the Martin Luther Kings are for today. Why don't we seem to have any of those deep thinkers and ethical heroes anymore? The answer to that is complex, but it certainly has much to do with the shape and strength of the whole mainline Protestant movement. It's difficult to generate giants from a movement that is itself anemic. But "where have all the heroes gone?" is not the right question anyway. And waiting for new heroes or new messiahs who will change the public face of mainline Protestantism may be a long wait.

Another way in which the adaptive challenge of the church's role in public life is reduced to a technical problem happens when we imagine that, if we allocate more money to social-action or social-justice programs, we will have met the challenge. Generally, such ventures reflect the assumptions and styles of Christendom and the modern era. Simply putting more money into old or established vehicles and agencies will not address the challenge. As with other adaptive challenges, the people facing the challenge have to do the work. Leaders will help the people in congregations and denominations of the Protestant mainline engage in this work. They will ripen the challenge and prepare people to engage it; they will help to name and frame the challenge in accurate ways; and they will manage distress as we engage in learning and change, loss and risk.

For Reflection and Discussion
- How do you react to the topic of "the church and the public square"? Does it excite you? Distress you? Engage you?
- I have said that the search for new giants or heroes represents a technical fix for what is an adaptive challenge. Does that make sense to you? Why or why not?

The Church and the Public Square: Where Things Stand

Before we can talk usefully about the church and the public square to-day, it is important to take a brief look backward, to see where we have been and how things have changed leading up to the present moment, these early years of the twenty-first century. It seems safe to say that, during the era of American Christendom, the Protestant mainline de-nominations enjoyed a dominant role in the public life of America. Ro-man Catholicism was largely viewed as a faith of immigrants, and, while the Catholic Church did play important roles, those roles tended to fo-cus on the life of Catholic parishioners and parishes. For a time, Protestant-Catholic-Jew (in Will Herberg's famous late 1950s formula-tion) appeared to be a new American religious establishment. But this new arrangement seemed to fracture soon after it was announced. Ju-daism continues to be a significant presence in America, but often the Jewish public presence is simply equated, rightly or wrongly, with sup-port for the nation of Israel. During that time, conservative Protestants did not tend to participate actively in the public square. While there were certainly exceptions, it was broadly true that conservative Protes-tants focused on saving souls and thus avoided politics. Mainline Prot-estants served, by and large, as the voice of a public or national moral conscience, and they led efforts to serve those in need. Their leaders en-joyed public prominence as well as the confidence of public officials, in-cluding mayors, legislators, and governors.

Much — one might say "everything" — has changed in the last fifty years, as American Christendom has, at least in its mainline Protestant form, declined and dissolved. Most mainline Protestant denominations have experienced a forty-year or longer decline in numbers of mem-bers, churches, and influence. In addition, the many institutions that were part of the mainline Protestant world, such as colleges and univer-sities, various men's and women's associations, lodge and service groups, YMCAs and YWCAs, have either loosened their ties to the churches and denominations that founded them or have themselves faded.

While the mainline churches have lost numbers and clout and in many cases been afflicted with chronic and disabling conflict, a new form of highly conservative Protestantism has emerged in congrega-tions and on the airwaves across America. This new form of conservative Protestantism, often referred to as "the Christian Right," has some family resemblance to historic evangelicalism, but it is also a different phenomenon in many ways. One might suggest the difference by pointing to the difference between Billy Graham and Pat Robertson. Graham was a traditional evangelical who focused primarily on personal religion and salvation. His venues were huge stadiums where he would hold services night after night for a week, the whole thing modeled on the uniquely American experience of the revival. By and large, Graham avoided social and political issues, though in his older years his comments on such matters emphasized compassion and tolerance.

By way of contrast, Pat Robertson's venue is the television studio and his popular program "The 700 Club," as well as his Christian Broadcasting Network. Robertson speaks about personal salvation, as Graham did, but he goes far beyond it to declaim on a host of hot-button political issues, including abortion, homosexuality, Islam, and American foreign policy and military power. Robertson represents the new Christian Right, which is really quite different from traditional evangelicalism. Along with the late D. James Kennedy of Coral Ridge Ministries, James Dobson of *Focus on the Family*, and Tim LaHaye, author of the enormously popular *Left Behind* series of best-selling books and movies, among others, this segment of evangelicalism in America has morphed into something that has many of the earmarks of a new American fascism. It merges religion and American nationalism and defies the Constitution's principle of separation of church and state; it fosters hatred of perceived outsiders and enemies and stimulates a kind of group paranoia among its adherents; and it is intolerant of other religious faiths. This new militant presence of conservative Christians plays a very active role in politics, taking positions on matters ranging from statewide referenda and legislation to candidates for national office to appointments to the judiciary. These leaders, their churches, and their various parachurch organizations and media enterprises now play a major role in politics in America.

Meanwhile, Roman Catholicism has moved from the margins and its earlier immigrant status into the cultural mainstream. Nevertheless, Catholicism, like many mainline denominations, tends to be divided. Some highly conservative Catholics make common cause with the Christian Right on a range of political and cultural matters; other Catholics appear to have more in common with mainline Protestants when it comes to positions on ethical questions and the public role of Christians, with some notable exceptions, such as the issue of abortion. Evangelicals are also divided. Many identify with the Christian Right and are tacitly supportive of their political stances, if not active supporters. But other evangelicals tend toward a more progressive role, and they are critical of the Christian Right's embrace of the Republican Party. Evangelical leaders such as Bill Hybels and Rick Warren have spoken out about AIDS, global poverty, and climate change, incurring the disapproval of Christian Right leaders such as Dobson and the late Jerry Falwell.

The dominant options for the church in the public square have tended to be either a new triumphalism or a tongue-tied quietism. In using the word "triumphalism," I am speaking of a Christian Right that promotes the idea that American was and is a "Christian nation." By falsely rewriting history in this way and through its political activism, the Christian Right seeks to restore its imaginary picture of that pristine Christian America past. Its agenda is reflected in efforts to make abortion a criminal act, to outlaw the civil rights of gay people, to "protect" marriage, restore prayer to the public schools, promote sexual abstinence, limit immigration, and other legal and social ventures that they identify as "family-values" issues. Theirs is an effort to write their version of Christianity into law as well as to instill it in the mores of American culture. The triumphalist political agenda of the Christian Right is supported by a theology that trades in moral absolutes and has no room for ethical ambiguity.

Meanwhile, mainline Protestants have been, in many ways, marginalized and tongue-tied. "Tongue-tied" may be a bit of an overstatement, but it does seem accurate to say that mainline congregations and denominations, if they have ventured into the public square, have commanded little notice. Some have, for understandable reasons, chosen to emphasize the internal life and the ministries of their congregations, and thus have, in a role reversal, avoided political or social questions and issues. Others, perhaps the majority, have pursued tactics that may have been effective in the Christendom era but certainly appear less than compelling today. Such tactics include passing resolutions on social and political matters at regional and national meetings and then directing those resolutions to elected leaders and bodies. Many mainline groups have maintained — also in line with the strategies of an earlier time — a lobbying presence in Washington, D.C. These lobbying efforts directed toward national legislators, though not necessarily wrong, are seldom backed by the electoral or fund-raising clout that commands attention and action. What these churches and denominations have not done, by and large, is make effective use of television, radio, or the internet, a subject to which I will return.

Finally, in recent years there has been an effort to gather formerly mainline groups together with newer, more liberal groups from other faith communities or religions under the banner of "Progressive Religion" or "Progressive Christianity." Such efforts represent an important effort to find a new voice and exercise a new presence in the public square. But it concerns me that aspects of this movement tend to place their emphasis more on a progressive or liberal political agenda than they do on the Christian faith. There is a danger that "Christian" or "religious" is an afterthought or an appendage to another agenda or set of priorities. Another way to put this concern is to say that the attempt to create a Christian Left or a Christian Progressive movement to offset the Christian Right may unwittingly accept the terms of engagement established by the Christian Right rather than reframing the issues and the conversation. Too often this sounds like recent Democratic Party efforts against the Republican Party, which can be summarized as "whatever they are for, we are against."

In the end, the capacity of mainline Protestant churches to play a leavening role in the American public square has a great deal to do with their own vitality or lack of it. That, of course, is the overall concern of this book and this entire series of conversations. If the churches that I have led and for which I wish to express a vision are to exercise serious influence, we will have to go beyond choosing sides in the current culture wars in America.

New Engagement in the Public Square

In the balance of this conversation I will put forward seven proposals to guide new engagement in the public square by congregations and leaders in the mainline Protestant tradition. I do not offer these seven as an exhaustive list, even less as a program or series of steps in a program. They are, however, themes that I view as urgent and as part of an overall response to the question of the church's engagement in public life as we face the adaptive challenge posed by the end of American Christendom.

1. Coming to Grips with Cultural and Religious Pluralism

A central characteristic of our new time, both in North America and globally, is religious and cultural pluralism: that is, in the place of one predominant worldview or religion, there are many. This is part and parcel of the postmodern world. When I was a boy in mid-twentieth-century America, the knowledge we acquired of other great world religions — for example, Buddhism, Islam, Hinduism — was chiefly from books. These were people and religions of other nations, other parts of the world. That is no longer the case. Where I live, the Pacific Northwest, one's neighbors are about as likely to be Buddhists or Muslims or persons of no particular religion as they are to be Christians. And this is true of San Francisco, Toronto, Chicago, New York, and most of the major cities of North America. As I mentioned in the first conversation, with the dawning of the twenty-first century, in some areas there were more Muslims in the United States than Presbyterians, more Buddhists than Methodists. This new religious pluralism is the backdrop to questions of public engagement.

As is usually the case, the two extreme options in response to this new pluralism are clear. One response treats all faiths and spiritualities as being of equal merit, and the choice between them is of no greater significance than the choice between Thai, Italian, or Ethiopian restaurants. The response at the other extreme is the declaration that there is only one right and true religion, and adherents of all other faiths are damned. I find neither option compelling or adequate in our new time: the first lapses into relativism, the second into totalitarianism.

We urgently need a third way, a way that will strive to develop an appreciative understanding and respect for our neighbors' faiths — and for those who practice them. As Jesus welcomed the stranger and "the other," twenty-first-century Christians must also learn to welcome those of other faiths and cultures, learning from them and with them. At the same time, we must know and respect our own faith and tradition sufficiently to engage in meaningful public dialogue. We should help people in our Christian tradition know what is distinctive about their own faith and its practice. A third way of being religious and Christian in a pluralistic society will be centered yet open: centered in the great core convictions of the Christian faith, yet open to the insights, experience, and corrections of others with whom we share life in community and in the public sector.

One implication of such a posture is that congregations and leaders advocate for the study of religions in high school and university curricula, particularly the so-called great religions of the world. The curricula in most public schools today won't touch religion with the proverbial ten-foot pole because of its perceived potential for conflict. Of course, this is not an altogether unrealistic worry! But the upshot is that Americans are increasingly illiterate when it comes to religion. We know little of religious faiths other than our own. And if we have no faith of our own, we know little of religion at all — its history, role, and contemporary influence in North America and throughout the world. In these educational ventures it is important to distinguish between teaching *about* a religion and teaching a person *to be* religious in a particular way. It is the proper business of churches, temples, mosques, and synagogues to teach people how to be religious in a particular way, that is, to practice their particular faith. The appropriate role of such communities is to form people in a faith. Public schools and universities have a different role: not to *form* people in a particular faith, but to *inform* students about religion just as they would inform them about other areas of life, such as politics, economics, or the arts. Our society's broad failure to teach about and study religion has contributed to the increase of fear and intolerance, not to mention a tone-deafness to religion in American media and in American foreign policy.

Beyond this general educational proposal, congregations and their leaders need to come to grips with the religious pluralism of our culture and of our world. They need to have an operative and articulated theological perspective when it comes to pluralism and other religions. Staking out an alternative between "different strokes for different folks" relativism and "my way or the highway" exclusivism is ground that mainline Protestants should occupy in the public square.

For Reflection and Discussion

- Does "centered but open" seem to you a helpful alternative or third way?

- How do you feel about the idea of advocating for the study of religions in the public schools?

2. Being Church in a Pluralistic Culture

The end of American Christendom and the emergence of a religiously pluralistic culture has another more specific implication. It means giving up on the "Christian America" project that was a strong theme of the mainline Protestants during Christendom, and that has now been taken up in a more militant form by the Christian Right. It is not our job to turn America into a Christian nation. It is our job to be the church, and to be, in the words of Jesus, "salt to the earth" and "light to the world" (Matt. 5:13-14). When religious people care more about the corridors of power than the precincts of prayer, watch out! Religion wrapped up with political power has demonic potential.

New Testament scholar Leander Keck spells out the implications of this for our time: "Put simply, the mainline churches must free themselves from the notion that they have a God-given responsibility for society, and instead claim the freedom to be influential participants in society by being first of all accountable to the gospel."[1] The implication of Christendom, with its de facto establishment of mainline Protestantism, was that leaders and members of such denominations perceived themselves to have both a right and a responsibility to run the show. The upshot of this is what I call "civic faith": this is a blend of good citizenship, middle-class morality, and golden-rule Christianity. There's nothing wrong with this compound as far as it goes; it simply doesn't go far enough. It doesn't go far enough into Christian faith and life to really transform lives; and it doesn't go deep enough into the Christian faith to make a distinctive contribution to American society. Moreover, the presumption that mainliners have both a right and responsibility to run society means that we have often neglected the church itself. And thus we have the sad situation of countless small, aging, and struggling congregations faced with relentless appeals to do good works in the community or to take a stand on some matter of public policy or legislation, but without the urgently needed spiritual formation and faith re-

---

1. Leander E. Keck, *The Church Confident* (Nashville: Abingdon, 1993), p. 79.

newal. To use the biblical metaphor of fruits and roots: many in the mainline have pushed for constant fruits, while they have neglected the roots. Therefore, it should be no surprise that the plant itself looks spent and depleted.

Keck's insight — and not his alone — is that churches and their leaders in a postmodern and pluralistic society will make their best contribution to the larger society by paying attention to their own distinctive qualities and particular gifts, by being centered yet open communities of Christian faith, and by being, as he puts it, "first of all accountable to the gospel." There is a certain paradox here. In postmodern times we are likely to contribute most to the larger society by being more deeply engaged in our own particular faith and tradition.

One implication of this is that, even as we advocate for people in our society to become better informed about religion and religions through public education, we need to do a better job of spiritual and Christian formation in our congregations. Again, this is the overall emphasis and focus of this book: strengthening mainline Protestant congregations, not so that they become enclaves apart and unto themselves, but that they may become a "light to the world" and "salt to the earth." Keck captures this in his call to become "influential participants." We are but one contributor to the public conversation and community, but our influence will be a reflection of the depth and integrity of our leaders and of the vitality of our congregations.

For Reflection and Discussion
- The proposal in this section is that churches will make their best contribution to the community by being faithful and vital congregations and Christians. In other words, instead of eroding what is distinctive about us, we claim what is unique and distinctive. What are your reactions to this theme and this way of engaging the pluralistic world?

---

3. Going Deeper

Earlier I cited Marilynne Robinson, the Pulitzer-Prize-winning author of the novel *Gilead,* and her trenchant observations about the intellectual rigor — or lack of it — in contemporary Christianity. After observing that there has been a "rise in this country of a culture of Christianity that does not encourage thought," she continues: "I do not intend this as a criticism of the so-called fundamentalists only, but more particularly of the mainline churches, which have assiduously culled out all traces of the depths and learnedness that were for so long among their greatest contributions to American life. Emily Dickinson wrote, 'The abdication of Belief/Makes the Behavior small.' There is a powerful tendency also to make belief itself small, whether narrow and bitter or feckless and bland, with what effects on behavior we may perhaps infer from the present state of the Republic."[2]

The words "narrow and bitter" she clearly aims at "the so-called fundamentalists," while she assigns the equally damning terms "feckless and bland" to the so-called liberals or mainline churches. The point is that we have been guilty of surface- and strip-mining a tradition that is rich, complex, and deep. Too often churches and clergy, in their attempts to reach potential new members or to satisfy the members they have, have embraced the silly, the insubstantial, and the trivial. It's one thing to become "as a child" to enter the kingdom of God; it's another thing to behave in a childish way. It's one thing to strive for accessibility in sermons and teaching; it's another thing to abandon substantive content altogether. What bedevils much of mainline Protestantism today is a depressing combination of sentimentality and the dumbing-down of historic Christian faith and conviction, with the result that a faith that has formed and reformed worlds and worldviews too often seems trivialized.

How has such a situation come to be? I fear that it has much to do with the kinds of people who have been attracted to ordained ministry in the last several decades, as well as the training they have experienced in the seminaries. While it's true that many such individuals are highly able, too many seem to be drawn to the ministry primarily as a way to care for emotionally needy people. Indeed, in the mainline churches the pastoral-care movement has so taken over that the once strong traditions of the teaching pastor and the preaching minister have been eclipsed. We no longer seem to have "preachers," only "pastors." We have often neglected a serious teaching ministry in favor of construing the ordained mainly as members of the so-called helping professions. In many instances, preaching has no longer been the strong center of Protestant worship; instead, the church has evolved into "a caring community."

2. Marilynne Robinson, "'Hallowed Be Thy Name'?" *Harper's* (July 2006): 20.

There is certainly nothing wrong with genuine caring; it is a part of Christian faith and life, but not the whole of it. Without the nourishment of serious thought and study, caring tends to become cloying and indulgent. It tends to reinforce the tendencies of congregations to become ingrown. One symptom of this is that many congregations have lost the strong, the able, and the adventuresome. There has been such a focus on needy people that, unless a person is willing to construe herself as either a care-receiver or care-giver, she seems to have no place in the church any longer! The message has too often seemed more like "let us take care of you" than asking that people "grow and grow up in Christ." It is largely up to the clergy to communicate a different understanding of their calling, and thus of the purpose of the church itself: our purpose is not to be caring or to be "like my family"; rather, it is to grow Christians, followers of Jesus Christ, and to engage the culture as people who are accountable to the gospel. It will take courage to return the pulpit to the center of focus and to reclaim a serious teaching office. But it can be done. Moreover, if people in congregations are to be equipped for a vital role in the public world, such a shift in emphasis and priority is essential.

Part of the diminution of the historic Christian faith and theology in the mainline has been a failure to deal seriously with evil and sin; there is a tendency to repeat more positive words, such as "love" and "compassion." Good biblical words and concepts such as "peace" and "justice" are often turned into a kind of chant or mantra, and this diminishes the complexity and depth of those concepts and realities. There is simply too much sin and evil in our world for people to take seriously a church and its message that does not seem to take account of these destructive realities. Life is hard and tragic, and people both encounter evil and commit evil. Too often the church seems to have bracketed out a serious consideration of these realities and indulged in a very sentimental distortion of the Christian faith.

In seeking to engage these challenges, I have urged that a congregation's capacity to understand, articulate, and use core Christian convictions is critical to its health and vitality.[3] If you don't know who you are

---

3. See Anthony B. Robinson, *What's Theology Got to Do with It? Convictions, Vitality, and the Church* (Herndon, VA: Alban Institute, 2006). In the course of this book I explore core Christian convictions in a way that I intend to be both accessible and challenging.

and what you believe, as well as what you stand for, you're going to be in trouble; you are certainly not going to be very effective as a church. In my view, we need congregational ministers to view themselves as theologians-in-residence who bring core Christian convictions and principles into continuing dialogue with congregational life and the wider culture. We need to rely less on the theological products of academia, which are often too specialized or abstract, and more on pastors as theologians. While some academic scholars make very helpful contributions, there is often a gap between what professional theologians produce (having their peers in the academic guilds in mind) and what the church needs and will find helpful. Congregational ministers who understand their roles to be theologians-in-residence should not pattern themselves after academic theologians; rather, they should engage the world from the standpoint of Christian thought and conviction.

A venture I have been engaged in for the last ten years is writing a regular op-ed column that is published in one of Seattle's daily newspapers. While I write about a range of questions and issues — political, ethical, and personal — I always try to speak as a Christian and to draw from the wealth of my Christian tradition. In other words, I try to bring Christian substance into conversation with contemporary issues and concerns in the public square. From Leander Keck's point of view, I try to participate in the conversation by bringing Christian conviction and perspective to it. I do not attempt to write as a general religious person or in the name of universal values; nor do I view religion or Christianity as restricted to the personal or private realms of family and feelings. It has been my experience that readers find this contribution engaging and worthwhile, and that seems to be true for Christians, persons of other faiths, and persons of no faith. One thing these columns have certainly provided: a witness to the fact that there are Christians out there who are not followers of the Christian Right. I got started in this venture simply by sending guest columns to the newspaper; in time the newspaper invited me to become a regular columnist. Many clergy, and lay Christians as well, may enter the public square in this way.

For Reflection and Discussion

- Writer Marilynne Robinson accuses mainline Christianity of being "feckless and bland." What do you think?
- I have argued here that "caring" has eclipsed "challenge," that "pas-

tors" have replaced "preachers." What indications do you see to support or contest this argument?

---

4. Recognizing a Current Danger

Over the last thirty years, a new variety of faith and politics has come to exert great influence. Dubbed the "Christian Right" by many, or the "Dominionist Movement" by others, it has insinuated itself into Congress, the White House, local school boards, and state legislatures. The Dominionists do have as much right to lobby and to be elected as anyone else does. That's not the point. The point is that this movement has totalitarian and fascistic characteristics: they demand an acceptance of their views and activities by other American Christians that they are not prepared to extend to others. My point in this chapter is that Christians of the historic mainline tradition need to be alert and prepared to critique and engage them.

Who are the Dominionists? They are not, by any measure, identical to evangelicals. They combine conservative, militarist patriotism with a selectively literal view of biblical interpretation and a triumphalist view of the history of Christianity. They do not permit questions or disagreement, and they oppose tolerance. They do not hesitate to consign those who do not share their views to both eternal and temporal damnation. Some of their media leaders are Pat Robertson and the Christian Broadcasting Network (television), James Dobson and *Focus on the Family* (radio), the recently deceased Jerry Falwell (Liberty University) and D. James Kennedy (Coral Ridge Ministries), Tim LaHaye, coauthor of the *Left Behind* books and movies, the Trinity Broadcasting Network, and a half dozen other major leaders and media outlets. In addition, there are many local dominionist "wannabes" who are developing megachurches in towns and cities across the United States.

These media manipulators have transformed Christianity from a faith into an ideology. But faith and ideology are different. Faith means that there are limits to human knowledge and insight: we see and perceive, as the apostle Paul says, but not that clearly; we know and understand, but only in part (1 Cor. 13). To be a person of faith is by definition to acknowledge that there is a power and wisdom greater than we are. Ideology, on the other hand, claims to have the whole truth: it says that we as humans, because we can interpret the Bible ourselves, know the truth completely and with absolute certainty. Ideological groups believe themselves charged to establish their truth by whatever means necessary. Ideological versions of Christianity tend to look a lot like cults: they are built around male leaders who must be obeyed without question; they maintain hard and fast boundaries between who belongs and who does not, who is saved and who is not; they use fear to vilify outsiders and to enforce conformity among insiders.

Whether their influence will wane or continue to grow, I do not know. But it does seem to me that they represent a reality and a danger that other Christians must be fully aware of and be prepared to engage. Let me emphasize once again that simply dividing Christians into two groups, liberals and conservatives, will not help us. It will not help us here, particularly, to come to grips with the Christian Right. The Dominionists are not identical with all evangelical Christians, nor even all fundamentalists. In the end, it may be the evangelical Christians in the United States who will pose the most forceful critique and opposition to the Dominionists and their imperialistic agenda.

For Reflection and Discussion
- How do you react to the distinction between faith and ideology?

---

5. Going beyond Resolutions to Discipleship

As I have noted above, a frequent strategy of mainline Protestant churches for participation in the public square during the Christendom era was to write and pass resolutions on various social, political, and ethical issues, and then to dispatch these resolutions to their elected officials in the expectation that their views would be taken seriously and make a difference. Today, by and large, it must be said that they do not make a difference. The resolutions-and-pronouncements tactic has been overused and theologically underfunded. While there are times when some kind of public declaration of conscience must be made, it must be done sparingly. Furthermore, this is one instance where actions do speak louder than words. Instead of firing off statements, pronouncements, or resolutions to the corridors of political power with the apparent assumption that the occupants of those offices and hallways are waiting with bated breath for the church's views, congregations will be more effective if they emphasize the practice of discipleship. Disciples feed the hungry, build homes for the homeless, visit those in prison, love enemies, speak for the voiceless, and speak truth to power. The active practice of discipleship will do two things that the over-reliance on resolutions, meetings, and assemblies will not: it will change the lives of those involved, and those changed lives will be stronger, more credible advocates for the causes and the people they would serve.

The resolution format reflected the era of American Christendom, when the mainline churches had greater clout and understood their role to be, among other things, to serve as the moral voice or conscience of the community. In our new postmodern and pluralist times, our voice is one voice among many. We will not be compelling to our fellow citizens and elected officials because of our many words, but because of the witness of our lives. The instinct of those formed by Christendom was that the most important thing churches can do is speak on public issues. But effective speech and action on public issues is the outcome of sustained Christian formation. Our current dilemma is that we have too long neglected Christian formation — that is, making Christians and disciples — while prizing public action, and we have failed to see that the latter is dependent on the former. The bearing of fruit depends on our nurturing and tending the roots. The tendency to dichotomize social action and spirituality, or public witness and Christian formation, is a symptom of the overall problem.

6. Finding Allies in the Public Square

Typically, the mainline or more liberal Protestants have moved to their left when looking for allies for public engagement. They have turned to still more liberal religious groups, to civic groups, and to nonreligious or humanistic organizations. That's fine. However, I would suggest that we in the mainline churches complement this by learning to lean in the other direction, particularly in the direction of evangelical Christians. While some evangelical Christians do identify with the Dominionist viewpoint and strategy, many do not. Indeed, as evangelicalism has moved more into the American mainstream, more and more evangelicals are becoming engaged with issues such as worldwide AIDS prevention and care, poverty relief and the disparities of wealth/poverty, and global warming and climate change. Despite these developments in American evangelicalism, mainliners tend not to consider working with evangelicals, and perhaps the lack of cooperation goes the other way as well.

I believe that it is time to work at changing that. It can begin, of course, with as simple a step as building personal relationships with clergy and laity from differing churches. A recent project of mine has been to collaborate on writing books with an evangelical Christian, a biblical scholar who teaches at a university affiliated with the Free Methodist Church. We acknowledge our differences but tend to view them as interesting points for conversation rather than as deal-breakers. While he brings to our dialogue and work a strong Wesleyan and holiness perspective, I represent a more Calvinist tradition. He knows the world of evangelical churches and students; I know the world of mainline congregations and leaders. We have taught university courses and written books together productively, and I believe that we are modeling a relationship for others as well as being enriched by it ourselves. In this spirit, I encourage mainline Protestants to find allies among evangelicals as the old liberal/conservative polarity proves to be less and less useful.

For Reflection and Discussion
- Where do you and your church tend to turn for allies in the public square? Could you imagine building a relationship with an evangelical church or individual Christian?

---

7. Using the Media More Effectively

Mainline Protestantism was born simultaneously with the invention of the printing press. True to our origins, we have been people of the written word. We like hymnals, book clubs, printed newsletters, and all that kind of printed stuff. That's fine for those who came of age during the era of print media. But many people today operate either largely or completely in the world of the visual image: the computer or the television, and their corollary devices and technologies. Because fundamentalism has tended to be an oral culture and movement, it has made the transition to radio, television, and the internet more swiftly and effectively than have the mainline Protestants. Like it or not, the dominant forms of expression in today's public square are television and the internet. To be "influential participants" (Keck), we have to learn new skills and find new forms.

Some of us are beginning work in these directions now, but we tend to be hampered by our denominational histories and allegiances. During a time of shrinking denominational numbers, we would like to use such forms to raise our own denominational profiles. Alas, almost all the same denominations have been dealing with budget shortfalls and program and staff shrinkages in recent decades, with the result that few resources are available for being influential participants. Mainline Protestants need to figure out ways to produce quality television and other media programs without turning them into denominational identity promotion. Could there be more shows, something like PBS's "Religion and Ethics News Weekly" or NPR's "Speaking of Faith," that different larger denominations or even congregations could purchase and identify themselves with when they are broadcast in their area and market? A good deal of the success of many television programs has to do with an attractive host or a lead person who becomes the "face" of the show and its message. Why can't the mainline churches identify people for such a role and develop a quality product? Garrison Keillor and Krista Tippett of National Public Radio are naturals, but there are many, many other possibilities.

I am not an expert in this area, but my point is simple: the mode of conversation in the contemporary public square is through electronic media. We mainline Protestants need to figure out how to get on the screen, into the airwaves, and bouncing from satellites, or else we may as well be in outer space (which is pretty much where we are in the minds of the many who hardly know we exist). Not long ago I preached in a fairly large Presbyterian church. Their contemporary service, held in a gym, was being held simultaneous with a more traditional sanctuary service. When it came time for the sermon, it was broadcast onto a large screen into the contemporary service on a closed-circuit system. The pastor told me that when they started doing this, and he appeared on the big screen, the kids in the church saw him differently. He seemed more real — and somehow more important — to them. "I saw you on

TV," they shouted. In our society today, the reality is that if it's on television, it's real.

For Reflection and Discussion
- Can you imagine more mainline and moderate Christians cooperating to get their message on television or the internet? What would it take?

A Concluding Word

As I noted at the beginning of the previous section, it is not my claim that these seven themes and proposals compose a plan for engaging the public square on behalf of mainline Protestantism. My purpose in this chapter and conversation has been a more modest one: it is to suggest that becoming more influential participants in the public life of our nation is an adaptive challenge. We no longer live in the world of small-town American Christendom dominated by our churches. It's a new urban and ex-urban world, a new postmodern, post-Christendom world. Neither Christian triumphalism nor tongue-tied quietism are faithful responses to the adaptive challenges we face. Moreover, like other adaptive challenges before us, this will not be engaged in and responded to overnight. This will take time, but that is no reason not to get on with it today!

Death and Resurrection

Our conversations up to this point have focused on congregations that need renewal. Perhaps a congregation that needs renewal is one that has been on a plateau in mission and membership for a long time despite being surrounded by change and growth in its community. Such a congregation that is ready for renewal may have important strengths but has experienced a slow decline in membership, participation, and mission. Another kind of congregation that needs renewal may have been beset by chronic conflict and consequent demoralization, and yet the embers of faith, hope, and love are still warm amid the ashes. These embers could be fanned into flame. In yet another scenario, the preceding sequence of conversations may prove helpful to a new church start, whether that new congregation is in the planning stages or in the early years of its life. In these scenarios, we are talking about building on enduring strengths, fanning the still-warm embers into flame, or guiding a new sense of call and enthusiasm. In talking about death and resurrection in this chapter, I do not have any of these kinds of situations in mind.

Some congregations need to die. Some died a long time ago, only no one has come along and given them last rites, pronounced them dead, or signed the death certificate. This chapter is about dead congregations and congregations where dying may be the very best — at least the most courageous — step forward into God's future. I know that sounds awful. Americans are inclined to dread and deny death and to do everything in our power to fight it off. There is something to be said for not going "gentle into that good night," as Dylan Thomas put it. But as Christians we believe (at least in theory) that death is not the end and is not the worst thing that can happen. God is the beginning and God is the end. Death precedes a resurrection because, on the other side of death, God is still God. Just as the Israelites had to ask themselves what it means to be Israel in the midst of exile, when land, king, and temple are gone, so mainline Protestant congregations, in their own kind of exile, need to ask, On what does our life depend? Does our life depend on the gifts of God (land, history, buildings) or on the Giver, the Lord God Almighty? At certain times trust in God allows us to know what death is and to face it; and in some situations it is only by facing and naming a death that a resurrection becomes possible. Only by dying to what is no longer alive in our lives and in our congregations can we allow God to call us forth from our tombs to new life.

While I have begun this conversation by making a distinction between churches that are ready for renewal and those that are ripe for death and resurrection, that distinction is more definite in theory than in reality. In reality, even congregations that are going about the serious work of renewal will encounter some dying that needs to be faced and lived into. There will be moments when they will turn to their leaders and say, as the Hebrews said to Moses in the wilderness, "You have brought us out here to kill us!" Congregations that let go of their past golden eras or bronzed present moment to open themselves to the Spirit and reinvent themselves for a new time will find that at times it feels like a death and resurrection — not just the relatively safer sounding "renewal." Still less does such a transformation feel like "a natural evolution." So there is no real avoiding this central dynamic of the Christian faith and life: that is, death and resurrection.

Still, by using this distinction, I am saying that some congregations are able, by the grace of God and a lot of persistence and hard work, to be remade and renewed under the same name, in the same location, and with most of the same people. For others — well, the surgery has to be more radical. It may entail an ending, a closing down, a change of name, a change of personnel, and a completely new self-understanding and purpose. This chapter tells the story of three such experiences. All are interesting in themselves, all have wider significance and potential, and I believe they are all instructive to congregations in general. The point is that there are times when a death is not the worst thing; indeed, it may quite possibly be the best thing that can happen. This does not mean that there is not pain, sadness, and grief. In fact, there is often much of that. But there is also hope, because God is God. How do you tell whether yours is a situation that is ready for renewal or ripe for death and resurrection? This is not something I know for sure. But perhaps the case studies that follow will help you reflect on that question and come up with an answer.

Atop Beacon Hill

Beacon Hill is the name of a neighborhood in Seattle. Ships at sea in the Puget Sound to the west and planes in the air on the flight paths heading into Seattle-Tacoma Airport take their bearings from this high hill, which stands above Interstate 5 as that highway bisects Seattle. The main street of Beacon Hill is Beacon Avenue, and the once-proud Beacon Avenue United Church of Christ stood on that avenue where it intersects with Graham Street. By the late 1990s, the congregation had forty members on its rolls, but only about fifteen people were actively engaged, that is, attending worship, giving financial support, and participating in congregational life. The average age among the fifteen who were active was over eighty years old. Over the two preceding decades, the actual building on Beacon Avenue had become a home for many congregations: there were as many as seven different congregations, all of them small, who rented space and held their services at Beacon Avenue UCC. Some of the congregations were predominantly Samoan, others African-American, and still others Asian-American; some were mainline Protestant, one was a break-off Roman Catholic group, and yet another was Pentecostal. Such a heady mix was not surprising because, by the turn of the twenty-first century, Beacon Hill was the most racially and culturally diverse of all of Seattle's many neighborhoods. A less expensive housing stock made it a neighborhood that new immigrants had been moving into for generations.

The mix of congregations at Beacon Avenue church building was in many ways an exciting one. Furthermore, by 1990 the Beacon Avenue United Church of Christ congregation had come to see its open door to the many users as its primary ministry. Meanwhile, however, the members of the host congregation were aging and their own numbers were getting ever smaller. I should say, as an aside, that I have observed a number of congregations that embrace sharing their church buildings with others, both churches and other groups, as their ministry. It is a noble gesture, but describing it as "ministry" is generally not quite the whole truth. Usually, the many other users are renting space, and their rent payments are keeping the host congregation in the black, or at least keeping it from going too far into the red. At a deeper level, this arrangement enables a slower demise for the host congregation: death is staved off, but just barely. I can imagine a wonderful situation where different congregations share the same facilities in a true partnership and shared ministry. But when one of the congregations owns the land and buildings and the others rent from it, that dynamic alone tends to inhibit true partnership and shared commitment. The congregation that owns the land and buildings tends to become involved in a great deal of landlord-tenant work, which is not really the purpose of a church. In many cases that work would be better done by a property-management firm. The renting groups may be friendly and supportive enough, willing to have an occasional joint worship at Thanksgiving, but usually their commitment is a limited one at best. If they get a better offer, or grow large enough to build their own church building, they are on their way. It seems to me that a real partnership would be one in which all the congregations sharing the building(s) would have equal rights and equal responsibilities for the facility and the shared ministry. In the best of all possible worlds, the different congregations would all enter into the arrangement at the same time and on the basis of a carefully worked out covenant so that the playing field would be a level one.

The elders of the Beacon Avenue congregation — and "elders" is a literal description more than a church office or title — came to the conclusion, after the retirement of a beloved minister, that they could no longer carry on as a church. Being a landlord, keeping up the property, and dealing with the tenants was too much. The denomination's regional judicatory was happy to help them close; it was prepared to receive the property upon the congregation's closure and considered the possibility of developing it as a site for judicatory offices. The judicatory made a proposal to do just that. But that wasn't quite what the elders had in mind, and the congregation voted down the judicatory's plan. They were willing to see their church close, but they still wanted a church, preferably a vital and growing church that was part of the United Church of Christ denomination, right there on Beacon Avenue, atop Beacon Hill.

At that time I was serving as the senior minister of a larger congregation in downtown Seattle. Because I lived not far from the Beacon Avenue church, and because I thought it would be unfortunate for my denomination to lose its last foothold in this most racially and culturally diverse part of Seattle, I had conversations with the elders about whether or not my congregation might be of help. One thing led to another, and in 1999 we put together a planning team made up of equal numbers from the Beacon Avenue UCC and from my congregation, the Plymouth Congregational United Church of Christ, which agreed to provide both financial and leadership support. We pledged this support on one condition: that the Beacon Avenue Church celebrate its journey and ministry, call it a day, and close its doors for a predetermined period of time. After the closing of the old church, a new church with a new name, a new purpose, and new pastoral leadership would open its doors at that location. We proposed this series of steps for a couple of reasons: (1) the existing congregation had grown small and weary; (2) we studied the recent history of Beacon Avenue UCC and discovered that, over the preceding two decades, the denomination had put considerable amounts of money into Beacon Avenue UCC in hopes that it would grow in membership. They had tried different programmatic and staffing ideas, all supported by denominational funding and consultation. But the money had not translated into fresh vitality or into new and younger members.

Our hunch was that, instead of getting just a blood transfusion, Beacon Avenue needed something more radical: call it a heart transplant. All the parties, including the judicatory, Beacon Avenue UCC, and Plymouth Church, agreed to proceed on that basis, to develop a new church start plan that called for celebration and closing (death) of the existing church, a fallow period (further planning and discernment, plus the availability and provision of pastoral care for the former Beacon Avenue UCC members), followed by a new church opening (resurrection). The celebration and official closing happened in March 2000. The fallow period officially lasted eight months.

Going about it in this way meant a couple of very important things. It meant that the playing field of the new church was a level one for those who were called by God to take part in it. The message (one that can be communicated with all the best of intentions) was not: "Welcome to our church, where we have been members for decades and will tell you how things go here." Instead, it was: "Let's suspend old assumptions, start afresh, and do a new thing here." The same thing was true regarding the presence of the church in the community and neighborhood. It was a little like putting up Under New Management signs when the name changed and the new signs and banners went up. We went door to door all over Beacon Hill with a brochure and an invitation to the new church. The message was not "come join us"; rather, it was "Come, let us be a new church, a new *kind* of church together!" There's a crucial difference in those two messages: one builds on an us/them distinction, while the other leaps over such a distinction in favor of a new creation (Gal. 3:28). And that difference needed to go deeper than changing the church sign and hanging out banners. It needed to be deeply internalized in every aspect of the life of the new congregation.

Internalizing the reality of a truly new creation meant a number of things, including a new name, a new purpose/mission statement, and new leadership. It also meant financial support that would help the new church to not just limp along but to get up and run. Plymouth Church agreed to provide $50,000 a year for the new church start for five years (renewable after evaluation at the five-year point), along with providing some key leadership assistance and other forms of counsel and support. In doing this, the Plymouth congregation was renewing a role and ministry it had performed often between 1900 and 1930, the role of "mother church." In the intervening years, they had used other strategies for new church starts. This Beacon Hill initiative represented the reclaiming of an older strategy: a new congregation sponsored by an established one. It proved to be an attractive and exciting mission challenge for the members of Plymouth Church, even as they provided crucial support to the new venture. As we began, there would be five Plymouth members on the new governing board of the new church; they would join five members of the former Beacon Avenue Church, who were now members of the new church's board. This proved to be a good mix: the five newcomers had a fresh perspective; the five from Beacon Avenue had community connection. Beyond those ten, there would be the new pastor and one person from the judicatory, the Pacific Northwest Conference.

When it came time for a new name, the new governing board invited suggestions. Four or five promising new names came forward.

Dorothy, who had been among the elders of the Beacon Avenue Church (she had been its treasurer for forty years) and was on the new board, said:

"I went to my Bible, and I think we should call the new church 'Bethany.'"

"Bethany," another board member replied, "very pretty name — but Dorothy, why 'Bethany'?"

"Because," said Dorothy, "Bethany is where Jesus raised Lazarus from the dead. If this is going to happen, it's going to take a resurrection."

We prayed over the various naming options, but there never really was much question. It was — and is — Bethany United Church of Christ, because "Bethany is where Jesus raised Lazarus from the dead." The old name and sign came down, and a new sign went up. A new reality, a resurrection reality, was announced. The new church opened on the first Sunday of Advent in December 2000.

"What about the mission/purpose?" the board asked. This also required prayer, discernment, and study. The board was aware that Beacon Hill was the most racially and culturally diverse area in Seattle. That had to figure into the mission/purpose, as it did into the call to a new pastor. The new purpose statement reflected the resurrection theme of the new name as well as the setting of the church: "Our mission is to be and build a living and breathing, loving and serving, multi-racial, multicultural, intergenerational church on the corner of Beacon Avenue and Graham Street." One implication of this mission and purpose was soon apparent: in order to be and build a vital new church, the new congregation would need more than the one hour of access to the church buildings on Sunday, which was all that was afforded by the current arrangements with the other groups using the building. It wasn't an easy decision, but the board decided to reduce that number of renter congregations from six to two over a transition period of time. This opened up schedule possibilities and created space for a new congregation to grow. But this was not without risk either: making such choices meant giving up revenue for the church. This was like the situation of Abraham and Sarah when they gave up on the idea of going with Ishmael, Abraham's child by Hagar, but held out in the face of Sarah's impossible barrenness for the fulfillment of God's promise in a child born of Abraham and Sarah.

During the spring and summer of 2000, the governing board of the new church did a pastoral search. After considering several candidates, the board called a Taiwanese-American woman who was ordained in the Presbyterian Church (PCUSA) and lived and worked in Seattle. Angela Ying had the right mix of gifts and strengths for the challenging work of being a new church start pastor. Furthermore, her own ethnicity signaled the identity of the new church. Beyond that, it turned out to be quite helpful that she did not come to Beacon Hill from afar. While someone who did come from some distance might also thrive in the new position, Angela came knowing the community, and she came with friends who wanted to join her in this new venture.

Over the years that followed, Angela and her friends worked tirelessly to participate in and bring to fruition the new thing that God was doing on Beacon Hill. As of this writing, Bethany Church is truly vital, alive, and growing. There are over 150 members and 50 children taking part in the new congregation. Bethany is a significant presence in its neighborhood and in the city: it was recently featured on the front page of the *Seattle Times* on the Martin Luther King holiday. The congregation's racial/ethnic makeup is roughly a third Caucasian, a third African-American, and a third Asian-American. That is no small gift and accomplishment given the tendency of most churches in North America to be predominantly of one racial or ethnic group. Have there been challenges and problems? Certainly. Have there been successes and accomplishments? Absolutely. But one thing is clear: a resurrection has taken place on the corner of Beacon Avenue and Graham Street on Beacon Hill.

The initial decision not to renew the existing church but to close (let it die) and start afresh (resurrection) was crucial to the success of the new start. As I indicated above, the way its death and resurrection were planned overcame the often difficult dynamic of "longtime members" and their established congregational culture versus "newcomers." Everyone was a newcomer. Readers may wonder whether members of the old Beacon Avenue congregation took part in Bethany. Some did (about ten); some moved to other churches; and some, in the natural order of things, moved on to God's eternal presence. The new congregation and its leadership have been very clear about their mission/purpose and their identity. And this has also been a crucial ingredient in the congregation's new life and success. While a multiracial, multicul-

tural church is not for everybody, there are those who feel called —
even compelled — to be a part of such a congregation and ministry.
This focus gave Bethany a clear identity, one that is in touch with a new
time. In the era of American Christendom it was sufficient to have a denominational identity: to be the church of "our" denomination for this
part of a city or this neighborhood (remember Charlemagne and the
parish system). But, for the most part, an identity based on denomination alone is not sufficient in our new time. An identity or focus that
connects to people in the twenty-first century is crucial. It may be an
identity that is shaped by the church's theology or mission or by a particular ministry. Such an identity/purpose is what makes a church stand
out and stand up; such an identity/purpose is distinctive and attractive.

What did we learn from this experience of death and resurrection?
Perhaps there are three key lessons:

1. Some settings are beyond renewal, but dying can open the door to
   resurrection.
2. Clear purpose and identity are essential to a successful new start.
3. Strong leadership and strong support (from another church perhaps, as well as from the judicatory) are both crucial elements of
   success.

My own conclusion is that such a model may be useful in a number of
situations. When the existing congregation has grown small and elderly, and when that congregation finds itself in a community that has
changed radically, death and resurrection may be what God has in
mind.

For Reflection and Discussion
- What are the key things you learned from the Beacon Hill case study?
- What are your hunches about factors that make some congregations
  ready for renewal and others ripe for death and resurrection?

In the University District

This second case is different in several ways, and it is still in the planning and development stages as I write. So we don't know yet whether

it will become a reality on the ground. Another thing that is different is my own involvement. While I have been involved in extensive conversations with people engaged in this new venture, I am not a direct participant in this project as I was in the Beacon Avenue-Bethany story. But this is another story that appears to entail death and hopes for resurrection, albeit of a different kind from the previous case study. It, too, may be instructive to congregations elsewhere in North America.

The setting is the University District of Seattle, which surrounds the main campus of the University of Washington. Arguably, universities such as this one were the paradigmatic institutions of the modern era. They were research centers, sites of advanced scientific work, and hubs of rational analysis. Churches of the Protestant mainline denominations felt that a presence adjacent to such universities was crucial during the modern era; thus there are perhaps fifteen congregations located within five blocks of the University of Washington campus. Many bear names that testify to their neighbor and their focus: University Lutheran, University Baptist, University Congregational, University Methodist Temple, and so on. Several of the congregations remain vital and are sustained by substantial memberships. But many have declined from their glory days in the first half of the twentieth century. Though it is common for these large Protestant churches to have sanctuaries that seat a thousand or fifteen hundred worshipers, many of these congregations now have memberships of around two hundred, with fewer than a hundred in worship on any given Sunday. There's one additional factor by way of an introduction: for several decades many of these congregations have participated in community-service ministries together as partners. That is, they have had significant experience of working together for good chunks of time.

Yet, as the new century dawned, many of these congregations found themselves facing three kinds of scarcity: not enough members, not enough money, and not enough future. Conversations began about the future, particularly among six to eight of the congregations whose situation might have been described as "urgent." The congregations discovered something amazing in these conversations: considered alone, they were all experiencing several kinds of scarcity; in fact, scarcity was arguably their dominant reality. But together they discovered an abundance, and this abundance was of two primary forms: abundance in land assets and financial resources as well as riches in faith assets. Each of the congregations held its own property free and clear, because most of them had been founded in the late nineteenth and early twentieth centuries. Individually, each faced significant challenges in maintaining their existing and now overly large facilities with diminishing numbers of participants. But again, when considered together, they held land assets in the prized University District of well over $100 million in combined value. Beyond the collective value of their land assets, each congregation — whether Lutheran, Christian Scientist, Methodist, Disciples of Christ, or Baptist — also brought a particular tradition of theology and practice. Individually, they stewarded their own particular traditions and faith practices; together, they could be a center of many faith traditions and spiritual practices.

Thus was born the concept of the University District Ecumenical Parish. The working idea has been to dramatically rebuild one of the six church buildings and sell the other five. The new ecumenical parish would include one large sanctuary for the gathered worship of the entire community of six congregations. It would also have smaller sanctuaries or chapels for each of the six particular traditions. The new center would house the shared service ministries of the University Ecumenical Parish. And finally, the new facility would have room for retail space, a supermarket, something that is not currently available in the neighborhood to the west of the University. The supermarket's presence would be leveraged for additional funds as well as participation in building an ample underground parking garage.

As I told the project planners, the name "University Ecumenical Parish" does not seem sufficiently visionary or compelling. It trades on words and concepts that are important to many of the participant churches and their members, but they may be less compelling — or even understandable — to those the new church may wish to attract. Of course, that is a fixable problem.

A more significant challenge for such a venture will be to move beyond their effort to simply downsize and share resources in order to reduce costs for each of the participant congregations, to move toward something that is really new and has a powerful identity of its own. In this respect, this case is an instructive one. I imagine that increasing numbers of declining churches will have to consider some sort of merger with one other congregation, and that could prove to be only a stopgap measure on the way to their eventual demise. It would be better to accept the death of an old identity that was appropriate to an earlier time, and to embrace the rising toward a new identity and vision in a new time. I suggested just such a thoroughgoing transformation to the planners of the university parish; and I suggested that they consider names such as "Cathedral of Hope," or "Seattle's Urban Monastery," or "New Beginnings Faith Center." I don't claim that any of these is the right name, or even that they suggest the right purpose and vision. But they do point to something new, and they do suggest that there will be a death and a resurrection.

In addition to a truly new and compelling purpose and vision, another key to success in such a venture of rebirth will be leadership, as it was in the previous case study. I imagine that the temptation will be to create a leadership collective made up of the clergy and key lay leaders of the existing partner congregations. But I have a feeling that that would prove to be a mistake. There would always be the question: "Am I the leader of my particular congregation and responsible to it, or am I a leader of the new thing with primary responsibility for it?" Furthermore — and perhaps more importantly — leadership amid death and resurrection has to have significant capacity for seeing things in new ways, not to mention a capacity for taking risks. In such a situation, leaders will not only need a strong faith and a theological basis; they will need to be persons of an entrepreneurial spirit, something that has not been particularly evident among mainline Protestant clergy in recent decades. Again, the point is that leaders will need to spend much more time looking through the windshield at what's ahead than looking through the rearview mirror at what they left behind.

The University Ecumenical Parish, all things considered, does seem to me a promising venture, and it may be suggestive for other settings. It values the particularity of the different faith traditions, inviting each one to bring its own particular gifts and best practices to the new venture while entering into something truly new. Conceivably, such a parish would offer a rich tapestry of different spiritualities. At the same time, such a parish would have a common life and common ministry. The really key transformational movement in this story, up to this point, has been this insight: alone, each congregation had scarcity; together, they found that they had an abundance. That insight reframes the situation and is the key to a potential resurrection.

For Reflection and Discussion
- What insights emerged for you in reading the University District case study?
- What seems crucial to you if such a venture is to thrive?

A Third Death and Resurrection

We began this conversation with an actual situation, a congregation that has experienced death and resurrection atop Beacon Hill; then we moved to the University District situation, which is in the planning stages but is not yet real on the ground. The third kind of death-and-resurrection situation I would like to consider is not even in the planning stages; at this point it exists primarily in my own imagination. Still, I mention it here because I think it also fits the model of death and resurrection and has instructive possibilities for others. Moreover, it addresses a trap that many congregations have fallen into in the post-Christendom era: that is, the lion's share of their resources, both financial and human, are devoted to maintaining their buildings. While the responsible stewardship of facilities is certainly legitimate and important, when that responsibility overshadows everything else in a congregation's life, it is time to face some hard questions. The church building is a means to and instrument of church mission and purpose, but maintaining a building is not the end or purpose of mission.

I call this third death-and-resurrection model the "moveable feast." In the Christendom era, a congregation was known, in large measure, by its building and its location. Though we know better — that the church is the people — we tend to speak of the building itself as the church. And, as some know, the Greek word *ecclesia,* which we translate as "church," does not suggest a fixed building at all. *Ecclesia* means "the people called," or "the gathered people who have responded to a call." These were the people who gathered in response to God's call in Jesus Christ.

Is it possible that we are entering a time when congregations no longer have church buildings at all? Here's what I imagine: a congregation in a major urban area where real estate is impossibly expensive, a congregation that rents offices somewhere in that urban setting. The offices provide space for meetings, small-group gatherings, and a location for staff offices. Services are held throughout the city at different rented or borrowed locations. Those locations might be other churches that are willing to share their space; they might be theaters that are not in use on Sunday mornings; or they might be other kinds of civic halls or spaces that can be rented. While I am not involved in such a venture, I have read that something like this is going on with a rapidly growing Presbyterian church in New York City. It is a model that may be replicated elsewhere.

Again, a clear and compelling sense of mission/purpose is essential. Leadership is also critical. There is a certain death involved, because this does not look like what most of us expect church to look like. Where is "the church"? In a sense, it is a "virtual church": it exists in concept and lived reality, but without a concrete, wood, or brick structure or a fixed location. But a resurrection is at hand as well, as this kind of "moveable feast" congregation has the flexibility to take ministry to different neighborhoods and areas where the gospel needs to be preached, and where community needs to be formed and sustained.

For Reflection and Discussion
- Can you imagine a "moveable feast" church?
- What excites you about this? What concerns you about it?

Conclusion

Over the next fifty years or more, we are likely to witness significant changes in the way people do and are the church. Some experiments will fail; others will succeed. All of them — successes and failures — will have teaching and learning potential. While some congregations will be able to retool and renew in place, others will entertain — will be forced to entertain — more radical forms of transformation. It is my hope that this chapter can help us dream new dreams and see new visions (Acts 2:17), and to discover the God-given courage and strength to enable these new dreams and visions to become new realities.

Where Do We Start?

Our time together at First United Church had begun on Friday evening and continued through Saturday morning. After lunch the congregation was excused. The congregation's leadership group, about thirty people, stayed for a Saturday afternoon session with me, and as that afternoon session began, there were a few awkward moments. We had understood or assumed different things about how this final session would go. I thought that the leaders of First United would take the lead: the idea was for them to identify particular themes from my presentations that they would want to discuss further. Or perhaps they would "talk amongst themselves" about their next steps, and I would listen in and provide an occasional comment or observation. Believing that I had finished my time of presenting, I had backed my energy level down and was prepared to play a secondary role.

First United's leaders were operating on different assumptions. They anticipated that I would continue in the presenter mode, only now I would focus on their role and their next steps. During this awkward silence, they looked at me and I looked at them, each wondering when the other would begin. Finally, the congregation's president said to me, "We thought you would tell us what to do next." I'm sorry to say, I found her words irritating. This is what I thought to myself: "I've told you what I know. Now you figure it out. There is no easy recipe, no magic formula!" Instead, what I did say was this: "You folks are the elected and called leaders of this congregation, right?" They nodded. "During our time together I have heard you and the congregation say, in a variety of different ways, 'We long for spiritual renewal — for new life — in our church.'" They nodded again. "Well, I hope that my presentations over these two days have suggested some directions to you. Beyond that, I suggest that you here in this room, as leaders of the church, be the change you want to see in the church. If you want the church to be more spiritually alive and engaged, then do that in your own lives, your own faith, and in your leadership." I was really adapting to this situation the words of Gandhi: "Be the change you want to see in the world."

That was a good response, but not a sufficient one. In a certain sense, this whole book is a response to those congregational leaders' request for next steps. In this book I have tried to move through a sequence of steps, or "conversations," that are critical to reforming the church, particularly mainline Protestant churches, in the post-Christendom and postmodern era. Congregations and their leaders can, I hope, begin with Conversation 1 and move through Conversation 10 as a series of steps toward renewal. Yet the fact remains that there is no recipe, no magic formula, for renewal. This is true because congregations vary enormously — in their history, in their current situation, and in their strengths and liabilities. It is also true that change in human groups and organizations is not a technical matter. One cannot simply replace a few broken parts with new ones. Human groups are complex, and churches are, one might say, notoriously so. Moreover, reform and renewal are enormously challenging endeavors. An observation made by Lyle Schaller, seems apropos: "Many ministers give up too soon."[1] Reform and renewal require both time and persistence.

Nevertheless, the request of that congregational president ("We thought you would tell us what to do next") deserves to be taken seriously. Where do we begin if we believe that ours is a new time, that being vital churches in our new time requires reform and renewal? What is the first step? What are the next steps? Where do we start? I would like to respond to those questions in this concluding chapter. In addition to the sequence of these conversations, I will suggest five different ways or places to start, because congregations and their leaders are in different places. In some there is a high sense of readiness, even ur-

---

1. See Lyle Schaller, personal notes from lecture, Consultation on Parish Ministry, 1990.

gency; in others there is hesitancy, caution, and little real understanding of what has changed in our culture and why change in the church may be in order. Some congregations are soon to be or already are in the midst of a pastoral search process, which would suggest a different starting point. Deciding which starting point is right for you requires some discernment on your part. The following are five possible starting points, but you may come up with numbers six, seven, or eight on your own.

1. Start with Study and Conversation

Let's say that your congregation could be described as "sleepy": that is, no one seems to have any great sense of urgency. No one seems particularly given to thinking about questions such as "Where are we going?" or "Where do we want to be five years from now?" A friend has told me the story of his interview with a pastoral search committee at a small church in a Midwestern small town. Thinking to provoke thought and convey an impression of himself as a leader, he asked the group: "Where do you see yourselves [the church] five years from now?" They pondered the matter for a few moments and then said: "Five years from now? We expect to be here — right here."

When there is not a great sense of urgency among the members of the congregation, pastoral or congregational leaders could begin by gathering a group for study and conversation. The group might be an existing group, such as the church council, consistory, or session. Or it might be a new group that is made up of some elected leaders, some members who are new to the church, and some who could be described as particularly influential people in the congregation. There are advantages to either way of constituting the group. The former gives you a step up with the established leadership; the latter will plant seeds in different parts of the congregation, and it will give a pastor or other key leaders a way to "take the temperature" of a broader range of the entire congregation.

You can read and discuss some of the ideas in this book. In some situations, people may not be used to reading a book like this and may be reluctant or unwilling to do so. One alternative is to prepare brief written summaries of each chapter, distribute them prior to meetings, and begin each session by reviewing them. Several times I have referred to how Ron Heifetz describes what a leader is trying to do with a process like this: he calls it "ripening the work," or "ripening the adaptive challenge," and it means helping people come to a gradual awareness of the work before them. It means stimulating awareness, readiness, and engagement with the most important challenges facing the congregation — and doing so over time. For the pastor or lay leader who is ready to move forward on renewal right now (or yesterday), this pace will be frustrating. But that does not mean that it's unnecessary or unimportant. Creating this group for study and conversation is a way of ripening the work.

It is also a way for the leader to get a better sense of where people are as the conversations unfold over time. If the pastor has put together an intentionally mixed group, some longtime and some newer members, some younger and some older people, some in elected leadership positions and some "persons of influence," it will give that pastor or lay leader a good read on the congregation itself. Moreover, the leader will have gotten members in conversation with people who are not in the usual affinity group within the congregation. That will, in itself, stimulate fresh thinking and learning.

At the conclusion of ten weeks of study and conversation, the group itself may have come up with ideas for a next step. Or their question "How shall we build on and share this experience?" may be the focus of a concluding session. The next steps after the initial study and discussion may include any of the following options. By gathering a group like this for study and conversation, you are stirring the pot, turning up the heat just a little, and hoping that things will start to cook.

2. Start with Prayer and Discernment

Possibly a group has just completed option one; or perhaps there is a high degree of readiness, even urgency, in the congregation already: "We need to get moving." "We need to do something." "We want our church to grow, to be more alive, to make a difference!" If that's the case, you might consider starting with prayer and discernment, with turning to God and asking God's guidance about what is the crucial next step. Ask God to help you discern the *essential* from what is merely *important*.

Discernment is, of course, a particular spiritual discipline and practice. If you choose this option as a place to start, you will be well served by beginning with some teaching about the nature and practice of discernment. I have already mentioned several resources that provide guidance in this regard. Some congregations are experienced in discernment, but many are not. Particularly if the congregation feels a sense of urgency, the season of prayer and discernment may seem too slow for some of the members. In part, that is the point: while reform and renewal are urgent, you don't want to go off half-cocked. Loren Mead, founder of the Alban Institute, cautions against putting a $20 plant in a $2 hole.[2] In other words, prepare the ground, loosen the soil, make sure you have good drainage, and enrich the soil with compost or fertilizer if necessary. Prayer and a process of discernment are a way of preparing the ground. Seek God's guidance and the mind of Christ for how your congregation is to move into its future. Engage in a process of discernment using the methods described in *Discerning God's Will Together*, the excellent book by Danny Morris and Charles Olsen. Ask questions such as "What is the matter for discernment?" and move through the important steps of shedding, rooting, improving, and the rest that are prescribed by Morris and Olsen.[3]

The essential point of a discernment process is for us to make a serious and good-faith effort to do what God would have us do, and not simply what we want to do. The two may prove to be the same, or they may not. But the time spent in prayer and discernment will prepare the soil of our hearts and the nutrients of our minds so that what God plants there and what we nurture does stand some chance of flourishing.

3. Start with the Sermon

Sometimes pastors have considerable leverage, and sometimes they do not. In situations where a pastor doesn't have a lot of leverage, he or she may be rebuffed in trying to get the official board to study one book or another, or to have a conversation about the future: "We're too busy for

---

2. Loren Mead, *The Whole Truth* (Herndon, VA: Alban Institute, 1992), part 3.

3. Danny Morris and Charles Olsen, *Discerning God's Will Together: A Spiritual Practice for the Church* (Herndon, VA: Alban Institute, 1997), p. 21.

that." "That's not the way we do things here." "We've done that before." Those are just some of the ways such a rebuff may be expressed. If that's the case, the one thing most clergy get to decide is the topic for their Sunday sermon. So, if all else fails — or even if it doesn't — start with the sermon.

Most of those who have been to seminary have been exposed to the kind of cultural analysis that is found in our first conversation, "It's Not About You." But that doesn't mean that the members of their congregations have heard about it. Or if they have heard some bits and snatches here and there in the culture, they are unlikely to have put it together in any sort of synthesis or coherent framework. A preacher can plan a series of sermons on "our new time" that begins with a consideration of Christendom. A colleague of mine recently planned, with his staff, a Sunday morning service that they entitled "A Funeral for Christendom." Several different characters played by the senior and associate ministers offered personal words of condolence and remembrance on behalf of the deceased persona of "Christendom." One said: "Christendom, you were so great, and I really miss you." Another, a retired minister, said: "I'm angry that you've left us. I'm not sure who I am without you." A younger guy, skateboard under his arm, said: "I never really knew you." A woman said: "My parents loved you, but really I don't miss you all that much. I like where I am now — it's exciting." Whether a series of sermons on the end of Christendom and the new emerging era is done in a more traditional way or with the kind of creative imagination of my colleague's "Funeral for Christendom," ministers can use a sermon or a series of sermons as the first step — or the next step.

If a congregation is at a different point, a minister might do a sermon or series of sermons entitled "The Purpose of the Church." Such a series might look at a sequence of biblical texts, including Genesis 12:1-4, Matthew 28:16-20 or 5:13-16, John 20:19-23, and Acts 1:1-8. Each of these passages addresses the subject of purpose. A minister might also make use of the purpose-based typology from Kirk Hadaway's book *Behold I Do a New Thing* or the concepts in Rick Warren's *The Purpose Driven Church.*

Again, the point of such a series is to stir the pot and turn up the heat. The point is to get people thinking about those Peter Drucker questions: "What business are we in?" and "How's business?" It is to ask, Why are we here? What is our mission/purpose today? What do we need to do or be "on-purpose" as a church? Remember, when you start asking these kinds of questions and you engage in adaptive work, there will be resistance to and avoidance of the work. Remember, too, that resistance or work-avoidance does not mean you're doing something wrong; on the contrary, you are doing something right. Resistance and a certain amount of discomfort are indications that you're on to something important. One of the things that focusing on biblical and theological understanding of church purpose may do is expose the way a congregation has "displaced" its purpose, that is, has forgotten its true reason for being. As I noted in the chapter on purpose, congregations easily fall into the assumption that their purpose is to provide for their members' satisfaction and to comfort them, that is, to meet "customer needs."

A sermon series on church purpose might well be a way to work up to a governing board or congregational process to discern, articulate, and then to build on a fresh statement of church purpose. Spending time with key biblical texts will furnish the imagination of the congregation with images and ideas, and weaving more contemporary language and purpose statements into the biblical concepts will stir conversation and reflection.

4. Start with Purpose

It could be that the congregation's degree of readiness, its sense of urgency, is great. You are perhaps in the early years of a new pastorate and have high energy and enthusiasm; you have built trust with the congregants that has become strong; and some immediate and urgent challenges have been addressed (e.g., a new youth leader has been hired or a capital drive to renovate the building's physical systems has been completed). Now you are ready to start building for the long haul. You are ready to initiate a process of reform and renewal. At this point there is sometimes the temptation to go programmatic: "Let's begin this new program or that new worship service." "Let's initiate this ministry or that project." Such programs, projects, ministries, or services may be effective strategies for elements of the vision, but they need to be grounded in a clear sense of purpose. Otherwise, they are simply "things to do" that do not advance your purpose in a strategic way.

Does your congregation have clarity about a simple and compelling sense of purpose that is expressed in plain English? Can people say, "Our purpose as a church is . . ." or "Our mission is . . ." — and complete the statement in a sentence or two that really matter to them? Can they say, "The purpose of our church is to extend the reach of Christ," or "to grow people of faith," or "to be and make disciples of Christ," or "to be a community where Spirit and service come together"? Getting reasonable clarity about a compelling purpose is crucial to congregational reform and renewal. Such clarity becomes the basis for developing a vision (the three to five things we need to do in the next three, five, or ten years to make progress on our purpose). Programs and projects then become strategies that support the vision.

If this is your next step, to start with purpose, you may go about it in a variety of ways. As I suggested in the preceding section, you might begin with a sermon series. You might then move to a process of discernment aimed at a clear and compelling statement of purpose. That process of discernment could be something the whole church is involved in, or it could be something done by the governing board. Which direction you go on this has a lot to do with the style, history, and polity of your congregation. Generally speaking, it is desirable to have broad participation in purpose-and-vision creation as long as that process does not become too protracted.[4]

5. Start with the Pastoral Search Process

Let's say that your current pastor is retiring or has announced that she or he has accepted a new call. You are in, or soon will be in, a pastoral search process. Look for a leader. Look for a personality who is capable of good pastoral care, but someone who is not simply a chaplain, but a leader. Maybe at this point some candidates have more leadership potential than leadership experience. Depending on your situation and the demands of the position, that may be all right. But look for someone who seems to have the qualities and instincts of a leader. Those leadership qualities and instincts include the following: (1) they think in the longer term; (2) they tend to think in terms of systems and the relationship between parts and

4. Graham Standish, *Becoming a Blessed Church* (Herndon, VA: Alban Institute, 2005), appendix C.

the whole; (3) they have the capacity to motivate and inspire others; (4) they tend to emphasize things like purpose, vision, and values; (5) they appear to have the political skills and savvy to relate to multiple constituencies; and (6) they are *always* thinking in terms of renewal.

If your congregation is interested in reform and renewal, look for a leader; if the congregation is not interested in reform and renewal, and the members are pretty much dead set against anything that has the appearance of reform or renewal, do not look for a leader. Of course, most congregations are a mixture of hopes, desires, and expectations. We want leadership and we don't want leadership. If you are on the pastoral search committee and you decide to look for a leader, you need to do two additional things. First, you need to tell the congregation that you are looking for a leader; second, when you have found that person, you need to tell the congregation that they can expect a person with leadership gifts and orientation. In other words, prepare the congregation for the fact that their new minister is a leader and that is why you have called that person. Second, a pastoral search committee that is seeking a pastor who is a leader and not simply a caregiver, manager, or chaplain will need to be prepared to tell candidates what you need help in accomplishing. What do you need leadership for? You may say: "Our stewardship isn't so great; we need someone who will give serious and sustained leadership there." Or you may say: "We believe it is important to get clear on our sense of purpose, our mission, as a church. We don't want you to tell us what our purpose is, but we do want you to provide leadership as we gain clarity about a compelling sense and statement of purpose." In any event, the point is that, should a search committee say, "We need a pastor who is a leader," it will be important to go further and identify the challenges for which leadership is required.

So these are five important places to start:

- Study and Conversation
- Prayer and Discernment
- The Sermon Series
- Identifying Purpose
- The Pastoral Search Process

One might also add to any of these five the use of a consultant, or at least an able outside speaker. I often play this role in congregations just to get the ball rolling. We all seem to hear things more easily from someone who is not part of our congregation's ongoing life or relational system.

Starting at any one of these five points may lead to any one of the others. In other words, you may begin with either "Study and Conversation" or "Prayer and Discernment," and then move to a focus on "Identifying Purpose." Alternatively, you might begin with a sermon series that leads to a half dozen groups doing either "Study and Conversation" or "Prayer and Discernment." (If you go in that direction, careful selection and training of group leaders is a key step, so don't neglect it!)

If you start with or come eventually to "Purpose," and you are successful in developing a reasonably clear and compelling statement of purpose, biblically and theologically informed yet brief, then you can build on that by developing your vision and including in it either some of the adaptive challenges I've discussed in these conversations ("Stewardship as a Spiritual Practice," "Deepening Adult Formation," "Getting [Less] Organized," "The Church in the Public Square") or other pieces of adaptive work that fit your purpose. One further thought: the goal in working on purpose is in a sense twofold: you want both a statement of purpose and "a sense of purpose." These two are related but different. If you have only come up with a statement of purpose but have not animated a vital sense of purpose in that process, the statement of purpose will end up becoming some nice but meaningless words on paper that go on the shelf. On the other hand, some congregations have a strong sense of purpose — that is, people are energetic, willing to work and serve, and they want to make a difference — but they are moving in too many different directions. Such congregations will be helped by focusing their energies in a clear and compelling *statement* of purpose. Therefore, both a statement of purpose and a sense of purpose are necessary and are really part of what I mean when I talk about "Identifying Purpose."

For Reflection and Discussion

- As a starting point and next step, which of these five makes the most sense to you in your situation? Which of the five do you have the greatest energy for?
- How do you respond to the distinction between a *statement of purpose* and a *sense of purpose*? How would you evaluate the sense of purpose in your congregation? Is it high or low, vibrant, dead, or faint-but-still-ticking?

A Final Word: The Odd Couple

In this critical work of changing the conversation and congregational reform and renewal in our new time, there are two particular qualities that are absolutely necessary and yet not altogether possible, and so we have to rely on God's grace and strength. These two qualities are *urgency* and *patience.* Most of us tend to do well at one, but not at both. But we need both of those qualities in abundance for this work.

By urgency I mean: "This can't wait. We have to get on this right now, today, not tomorrow or next year." That sense of urgency should not be foreign to Christians. When Jesus came, he announced: "Repent, the kingdom of God is at hand" (Matt. 4:17). Jesus' ministry is suffused with a sense of urgency. "Be dressed for action and have your lamps lit," he said to his disciples (Luke 12:35). And he said to the crowds: "You know how to interpret the appearance of earth and sky, but why do you not know how to interpret the present time?" (Luke 12:56). In fact, urgency is such a constant theme and a consciousness in Jesus' ministry that it is surprising that anyone in his church should ever feel settled or comfortable at all!

Not only is urgency a constant in the Gospels and as part of the Good News, but our own times have their own particular urgency. It is common knowledge that mainline Protestant congregations have lost numbers of members, numbers of churches, as well as visibility and influence. While it is not my approach here to make membership growth the aim (membership or attendance growth is always a secondary effect of faithful ministry, not its primary purpose), we can't exactly ignore the numbers either. But, as I have sought to show in this book, the crisis is a deeper one than the numbers. They are a symptom. The deeper crisis is to take account of the end of American Christendom and the waning of modernity and to reform and renew the church for the time to which God has called us. With regard to the membership growth issue, I might say that my approach has tended to result in growth in membership and worship attendance and participation; but it is steady growth, not spectacular growth. All the congregations I have served have grown, but they have grown steadily rather than by leaps and bounds. My hunch is that steady growth may actually be healthier in the long run.

My own sense of urgency is a product of the gospel and of my reading of our times. I believe that the gospel is true and that the gospel is about saving lives. I am passionate about that. I do believe that the church as a whole and churches individually have a critically important role to play in the lives of individuals and families, of communities and of our society. And I believe that the reform and renewal of the mainline Protestant congregations and denominations is urgent.

And yet we must have *patience.* Change takes time and is slow in coming. The work of renewal and reform in response to the end of Christendom and the waning of modernity will last throughout my lifetime and probably throughout yours as well. People see and hear things in different ways and at different times, so we must be patient with ourselves, with our brothers and sisters in our congregations, and with our brothers and sisters everywhere. We must remember that "God's thoughts are not our thoughts, God's ways not our ways" (Isa. 55:9). What appears insignificant to us or by the standards of this world may be great and glorious to God. Moreover, we find ourselves living in a society that wants to do everything faster. Immediate gratification is not fast enough. All kinds of businesses and organizations push for short-term results and are more or less indifferent to long-term costs and consequences. We have fast food, fast lanes, kids who grow up too fast, and adults who are burned out because they are going so fast. In this driven world, patience is to be sought after, cultivated, and appreciated.

Patience in church life and leadership means that this is going to take time, maybe a long time. We will not make the shift from "established churchgoing" to "intentional churchgoing" (to use Diana Butler Bass's terms) overnight or even in a year. We will not make the transition, in Michael Foss's words, from "cultures of membership" to "cultures of discipleship" quickly or easily. This is why I have tried to emphasize, when speaking about various pieces of significant adaptive work (Conversations 6, 7, and 8), that all of these will take time. They are three-, five-, and ten-year pieces of work that will take patience, persistence, and time. Taking time does not mean saying, "We'll get around to it someday." It really is true that "it can't wait," and that "we do have to get on this now." And yet it will also take time for work to ripen, for loss to be acknowledged, for new learning to occur, and for the Spirit to work.

For all these reasons, what congregational leaders can reasonably hope for is not to arrive at a finished product but to establish and maintain a sense of direction. Like Moses, we may not get to the Promised Land in our lifetimes, but being on the way, having a reasonably clear sense of direction, and learning as we go are what we can expect and can be fulfilled by. To all my brothers and sisters engaged in the work of leadership, thanks be to God for your ministries. Don't give up! To congregations of faithful people everywhere who seek and serve the Lord in this new time, when so much has changed, thanks be to God for you. Don't give up! Take to heart the words of the apostle, words that hold together urgency ("the Lord is near") and patience ("let your gentleness be known to everyone"), and hold them close:

> Rejoice in the Lord always; again I will say, Rejoice. Let your gentleness be known to everyone. The Lord is near. Do not worry about anything, but in everything by prayer and supplication with thanksgiving let your requests be made known to God. And the peace of God, which surpasses all understanding, will guard your hearts and your minds in Christ Jesus. (Phil. 4:4-7)

Amen.

Index